Design Incubator

A Prototype for New Design Practice

LAURENCE KING

Published in 2013 by
Laurence King Publishing Ltd
361–373 City Road
London EC1V 1LR
United Kingdom
email: enquiries@laurenceking.com
www.laurenceking.com

A catalogue record for this book
is available from the British Library

ISBN: 978-1-78067-123-9

Printed in Singapore

Design Incubator
A Prototype for New Design Practice

Patrick Chia

Laurence King Publishing

Contents

INTRODUCTION

To develop new tools and to expand the possibilities
for the practice of design

More than a monograph of our projects and processes, this book is intended to be a handbook and journal containing stories of our adventures and case studies documenting insights as to where our ideas came from, how they evolved and how they developed. We give the reader some guides and clues as to how we do what we do and at the same time hopefully catch a wisp of the spirit and whispers that transpired between our studio walls.

The Design Incubation Centre (DIC) is a design research laboratory based at the Division of Industrial Design at the National University of Singapore, and a probe for the future practice of design. We develop tools, processes and capabilities and map out frameworks that are needed to engage in these new domains. Through our workshops, projects, initiatives and the development of new capabilities, we are able to engage and communicate the value of design to the different stakeholders such as other researchers, the industry, government agencies and policy-makers, while at the same time creating new collaborative networks for future investigation.

Our aim was and still is to expand the possibility and scope of how design could be practised, especially in the context of Singapore and the challenges and opportunities that have been presented to us.

Equally important, the Centre has always framed its activities based on their relevance to the Division of Industrial Design teaching programme at the National University of Singapore, and how it empowers the training of our students.

The Centre serves as a test bed for the teaching programme by hiring the students as designers and researchers, and engaging them through internships, workshops and involvement in teaching studio projects. We have first-hand insights as to how these young graduates and students apply themselves and this provides a valuable feedback loop which we can continuously tweak, adjusting our teaching methods to adapt to the demands of our changing landscape of design practice and to match the aspirations of these young minds.

Many of our projects and initiatives have evolved into frameworks and platforms which students and future graduates could then use as leverage to launch themselves into the future design landscapes. Many of the insights gained from this research and the experiences taken from our projects are used to inform the creation of new teaching projects, transferring knowledge, skills and subtle nuances in the process.

The Centre's approach and emphasis on the mining and discovery of unmet human needs enables us to continually redefine and reframe nascent areas of human interaction, daily life and social behaviour through the use of technology and software.

What we seek through this is the discovery of a new sensibility that aids us in the creation of ideas, products and services that augment human capabilities, and redefines the boundaries that exist between the physical and mental limits.

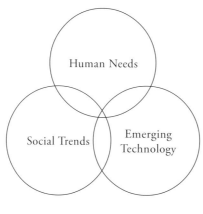

Areas of Interest

Most of the Centre's investigations are framed around basic human needs that might be constant in some aspects, but evolving in others owing to the advent of new or emergent social trends and technologies.

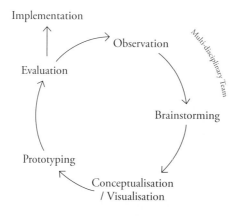

Design Process

This diagram above was adopted during our early years from a similar model employed by design consultancy IDEO in the book The Art of Innovation (2002), written by the firm's founder Tom Kelley. It was subsequently enhanced, tested and refined into a model unique to the Centre through its various workshops and projects.

With the realization that many resources and knowledge bases were stored within the various faculties in the University, we began to view the Centre as a means of engaging and mining from this talent pool.

Early on we also acknowledged that many key issues we were interested in taking on went beyond mere product and user experience design. Often the key problem and solution lay in the tweaking and adjustment of policies and, to that end, we have constantly sought to engage with relevant government stakeholders and policy-makers.

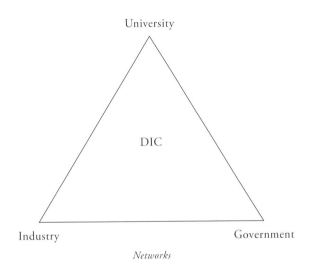

Networks

It was also important for us to engage with various industries, as it is within the domain of commercial production that the mettle of a designed product is tested, implemented and distributed for real impact on a user.

1 NEW ARCHETYPES FOR LEARNING AND PLAYING

Learning and Playing seem to be important and recurring themes in the Centre's research and investigation. This is probably due to the fact that my daughter was about two years old when I joined the Centre. Watching how she navigated in her environment and how she engaged with objects around her has provided a constant source of fascination and inspiration.

My daughter started riding a pushbike when she was about three years old; when she was about five, I bought her a proper bicycle with no training wheels. I remember vividly the first time she rode the bicycle: after orientating her with the pedals and the brakes, she was riding on her own, unassisted, in less than five minutes, without once falling off. I remembered when I was learning to ride a bike, it took me a week, and with multiple falls, cuts and bruises.

I realized that the pushbike provided a safe context in which she could be comfortable while pushing on two wheels and, over time, develop her balance gradually. She probably learnt to balance on two wheels without thinking or being conscious of balancing; to her, she was probably trying to move forward by pushing and walking with her feet. Hence, over time, she could move and hold her legs off the ground for a longer period of time, eventually gliding over greater and greater distances.

In the same line of thought—that the pushbike was the tool that bridged the gap—it seemed quite possible that the learning of any task, no matter how difficult, could be made simple and painless if we could break it down into parts or augment the learning with the correct tools.

On the other hand, I might also have robbed my daughter of valuable life experiences and lessons that could be learnt from falling down repeatedly for a week.

Many of our projects try to find a balance in creating tools that could help, without impeding, the natural cognitive and non-cognitive development of the child.

Playground Workshop

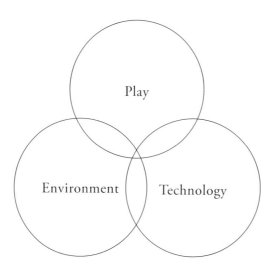

Context:

Playing and learning are integral to a child's development and providing good play opportunities helps children to develop physically, mentally and emotionally. Through play, children develop social skills, creativity and sensitivity. The Playground Workshop was developed with the aim of identifying new ideas of play through understanding a child's psyche, while examining physical acts of playing within different environments in Singapore.

Approach:

This three-day workshop sought to look at current play situations and to develop creative play solutions. It provided a platform for participants by drawing out diverse experiences from one another to explore existing play spaces and to analyze the motivational and deterrent factors that influence children. User observation was the focus of this exploration as we considered the relationship between children, play and playing environments. Through this process, participants also sought to discover new insights that could inspire new experiences, ideas and project concepts.

Workshop Documentation

Playground Workshop

3rd — 8th January 2007

Conducted by the Design Incubation Centre

Workshop Methods:

The objectives were to identify problems and form insights around existing playground designs as well as create alternative playground solutions.

Workshop participants are to explain the solutions developed with syntactic, pragmatic and semantic tools.

Step 1: Observe
Go out and see the world, gather subtle clues, and play!

Step 2: Analyze
Record field video reports of participants conducting investigative methods such as Body Storming, Role-playing, Behavioural Mapping and Fly on the Wall.

Step 3: Conceptualize
Visualize the final concepts and prepare a presentation.

Users

Children   **Parents / Carers**

Age   Involvement
Fitness level   Assistance
Personality   Audience
Height
Eye level

Equipment

Ambiguous   **Location**
Flexible   **Terrain**
Active/Passive   Equipment on Terrain
Fast/Slow   Height differences
Educational/Physical   Hot spots/Isolated   Scale & Proportions
Engaging   Spread the crowd   Sufficient activity space
Unexpected/Predictable Indirect control of movement   Allow a natural flow
Solo-operated?   Allow clear view for parents
                        Cool rest spots

BOUNDARY OF PLAYGROUND

LOCATION OF PLAYGROUND

Ideas   **Concepts**

Wind   A playground with a life of its own
Light   A fun space instead of a space with fun equipment
Bubbles   A game with the playground instead of its equipment
Moving Terrain   A more integrated placement of equipment
Sound   A fusion of the equipment and terrain
Partitions   A terrain with natural boundaries (wall and floor flows)
Rain   A playground with no ends (undefined boundaries)

Observations

Insights	Opportunities

Most stations cannot be enjoyed by kids in a wheelchair without some help from adults. Stations are either too steep or inaccessible by the less mobile.

Playground with wheelchair-friendly stations:
1 **Digger station**

Children's safety comes first. Parents will often be too worried about the kids to have as much fun as them. The upright position for play is easily accessible to adults.

Parent-friendly stations, where parents can become more involved in the fun:
1 **Two-sitter swing**
2 **Standing see-saw**

Popular playgrounds would include a combination of exciting (fast) and interesting (magical, constantly changing) stations. Popular stations would very often involve group play.
1 **Exciting:** speed & orientation variation, competitive, e.g. slanted merry-go-round.
2 **Interesting:** feedback, constant changes, e.g. water fountain.

Child-safe (hence also parent-friendly) playgrounds where parents need not worry about the safety of the child (e.g. inflatable playground):
1 **Inflatable playground for toddlers**
2 **Magical fountain**

Play can create a sense of achievement when you can do something your peers cannot.

Playground that emphasizes group play:
1 **Super-sized slide & see-saw**
2 **Merry-go-round**

There is an air of competitiveness. Maybe bringing indoor games outdoors can make the children want to play outside.

Bringing indoor games outdoors:
1 **Snakes and ladders**
2 **Mastermind**
3 **Giant cutouts on a huge box so that kids have to twist their bodies to the cutout shapes in order to fit in and pass through**

Directions and Concepts

Living Playground
Growing + changing
Parasitic
Landscape
Structured vs. unstructured

Effect Playground
Cause + effect
Unpredictable
Group play
Competitive

2D Playground
Intangible
Imaginative play
Lines + grids
Lights + shadows

Behavioural Playground
Explorative play
Understanding human
behaviours + habits

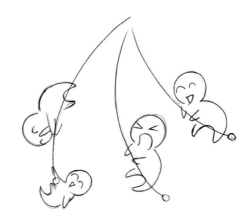

holes

Shadow play

light fountain

! ah!

soft jelly like bouncy

↑ pops up when 1 steps on previous "store".

jump trampoline.

bells.

Flooring

New Learning Scenarios Workshop

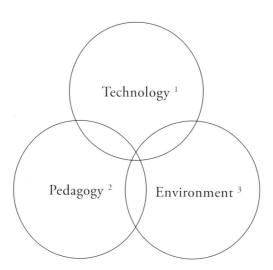

New Learning Scenarios covered three broad intersecting aspects:

1   It examined how emerging technologies could be integrated into the classroom as a tool to enhance learning.

2   It looked at how new ideas and approaches in pedagogy could influence the design of spaces and the way we might use emerging technology.

3   It explored how the spatial qualities of a classroom environment can be rethought and reconfigured to be responsive and conducive to the fluid and participatory nature of future learning,

Approach:

Facilitated by the team from the Centre, experts in pedagogy, information-communication technologists, education ministry officers, architects, designers and research students were brought together in a three-day design workshop to explore and examine how new possibilities and implications related to the fundamentals of learning might be questioned, formalized and realized.

Is there an optimal scenario or situation for learning?

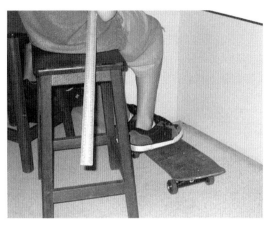

1

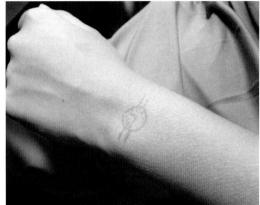

2

1 **Workshop Field Studies**
   Through field studies conducted at diverse locations such as schools and a
   gaming café, participants observed and took notes on the activities that took
   place. This method of direct user observation allowed the participants to gather
   insights into what children actually did and how they would behave. In this
   instance, a child was observed in a classroom fidgeting with his feet and moving
   a skateboard around; this behaviour, we later learned, actually helped the child's
   ability to focus on his task.

2 **Workshop Insight**
   The workshop participants observed that children enjoyed spontaneous and
   tactile ways of learning. Through moments of play or restlessness, children
   often use their imagination to create impromptu props to communicate their
   thoughts. In this instance, a child was observed drawing a clock face on his wrist,
   subconsciously expressing his concept and perception of time.

Experience Kaleidoscope

A personal and interactive experience diary for children

1

2

Background:

 The act of collecting, hoarding and sharing with peers seemed to be a social behaviour that children across age groups and various generations exhibited.

 With this observation, we studied the trends and objects that children have been collecting throughout history: bottle caps, tin toys, action figures, dolls, trading cards, etc. Building on this insight, we considered how the introduction of technology might significantly alter or create new ways in which children might share these experiences with their peers and adults.

Concept:

 The Experience Kaleidoscope is a learning toy device that builds on and enhances the collecting and sharing behaviours common in children. Instead of sharing physical objects, the Kaleidoscope enables a child to share recorded experiences and memories with his or her peers.

 The in-built digital camera module would allow a child to record and collect both images and videos of situations, scenes and objects encountered, while the projector module would enable the child to project these collected recordings onto any wall or flat surface when children come together as a group.

3

4

1   The experience of capturing and collecting their first butterfly.
2   Children sharing recorded experiences with each other by projecting the
    recordings onto a wall surface.
3   Finding and gathering experiences with friends using the Kaleidoscope.
4   Children peering through the viewfinder of the Kaleidoscope.

1 General lens
2 Set of image-capturing lenses
3 Rechargeable lithium-ion battery
4 CMOS sensor chip
5 Mini-projector
6 Removable flash memory
7 Micro-CPU board
8 Rotating knob activates Image mode or Projection mode
9 Rotational buttons to switch between images during Projection mode
10 LCD viewfinder and display

Toy Cameras

Background:

    During the prototyping process of the Experience Kaleidoscope, we discovered from our client–collaborator (a Hong Kong-based toy manufacturer) that a toy camera module is significantly cheaper than a video projector module. Building on this cost constraint, the team developed a new set of toy camera concepts that would effectively make use of and exploit the possibilities of these 'cheap camera modules'.

Basic Camera
An intuitive camera concept for children with basic photography, video recording and playback capabilities. The camera is housed in an ergonomic body casing with buttons made from wood. The rubberized lens cap acts as the on/off trigger, with the camera being turned on when the lens cap is pulled out.

Quick Prototyping

The team was interested in re-examining the way children's cameras were designed and we began by giving children basic tools and materials to allow them to construct the ideal camera that they would like to have and own. This exercise gave us insights into how children would create and use prototypes to express their ideas and desires.

WHAT DO THEY SEE?

WHAT DOES A HOUSEFLY SEE?

HOUSE FLY

GIRAFFE

WHAT DOES A GIRAFFE SEE FROM SO HIGH UP?

CHICKEN

HOW DOES A CHICKEN FIND ITS WAY WITH 2 EYES ON THE SIDE OF ITS HEAD?

What Do They See?
This particular idea, generated from an in-house brainstorming session, looks at using the
camera to perceive the world through the eyes of different animals.

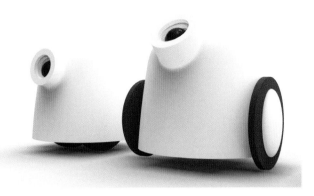

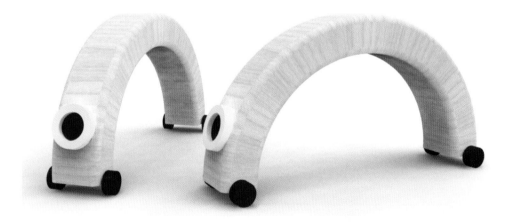

Toy Camera Concepts Designed by Children
These concepts looked again at the camera module as an alternative image- and video-
capturing device and how it might possibly be used for other kinds of play scenarios by
being the basis for a new line of children-designed toys.

Tomotomo™

Children's toy brand based around their play behaviour

Background:

Inspired by a lecturer at the university faculty who often brought her children to the office while she worked, the team sought to design toy objects or office furniture that could be sympathetic to both parent and child by acting as tools that could turn conflicting situations in the office into harmonious ones.

Tomotomo™ was a result of a few different project trajectories that were going on at that time in the Centre:

Office System Design

Play Objects and Ride-On Toys

The Workscapes Workshop

All three projects dealt with the idea of how an individual could reframe his or her definitions of working, living and playing spaces.

During that period, our client–collaborator for the Toy Cameras and Experience Kaleidoscope projects visited the Centre's studio and remarked to us that toys with storage capabilities had great market potential.

This spurred the team to focus the direction of the toy prototype developments by refining and creating a proper, fully fledged brand trademark, named Tomotomo™.

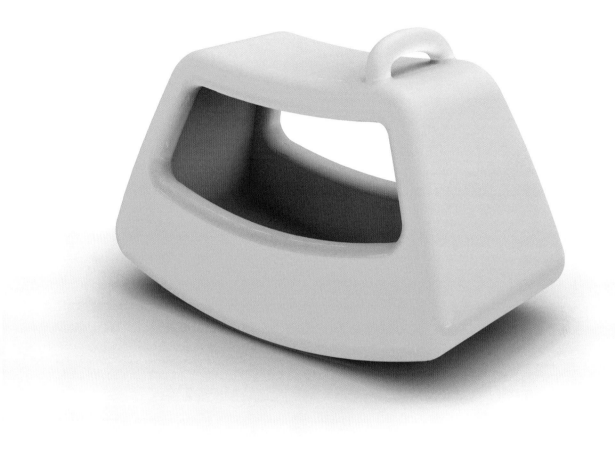

tomotomo ™

The brand:

> The Tomotomo™ brand was created as a line of furniture objects with storage capacities that children could also use as ride-on toys or playthings. Seeking to build unique relationships between play objects, children and their parents, the products developed under this brand will be framed around the playing behaviour of children.

Rocker
A rocking stool with an undercarriage storage.

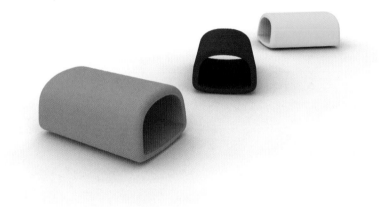

Trunkee
A rocking bench with hollowed-out storage space.

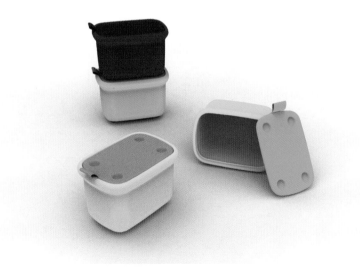

Stacker
Stackable storage which can be used as pull-along toys.

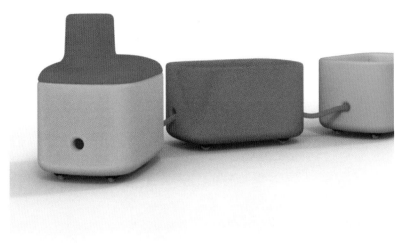

Choo-choo
A ride-on toy train that doubles up as a stackable storage.

Igloo Storage
Modular storage bin that can be combined to form an igloo structure.

Futon Rider
An indoor ride-on with removable cushions. The cushions are thrown onto the ground and when the child jumps from one to another, different musical notes are played.

THE TOMOTOMO IDENTITY
BASIC MANUAL

tomotomo tm

THE TOMOTOMO IDENTITY
BASIC MANUAL

Hello!

This is a work-in-progress version of the graphic identity manual of tomotomo.

With this document, we would like to guide you through the basic graphic identity of tomotomo.

DESIGN INCUBATION CENTRE

THE TOMOTOMO IDENTITY
BASIC MANUAL

Logo in Different Colour Applications

Below are examples of various forms of the logo depicted in different colours.

THE TOMOTOMO IDENTITY
BASIC MANUAL

Logo in Different Colour Applications

Below are examples of various forms of the logo depicted in different colours.

THE TOMOTOMO IDENTITY
BASIC MANUAL

Typeface

The typeface is an essential part of the visual vocabulary for creating a consistent look across a wide range of communications. We have chosen the typeface Futura for its geometric, playful, modern, legible and distinct typographic style. All covers of printed literature - stationery, forms, brochures, posters, etc. should use Futura.

Futura Light

abcdefghijklmnopqrstuvwxyz !@#$%^&*()""
ABCDEFGHIJKLMNOPQRSTUVWXYZ0123456789

Futura Book

abcdefghijklmnopqrstuvwxyz !@#$%^&*()""
ABCDEFGHIJKLMNOPQRSTUVWXYZ0123456789

Futura Bold

abcdefghijklmnopqrstuvwxyz !@#$%^&*()""
ABCDEFGHIJKLMNOPQRSTUVWXYZ0123456789

THE TOMOTOMO IDENTITY
BASIC MANUAL

Colour Palette

Apart from the colour of the tomotomo logotype, there are a few colour selections that have been set aside for the various toy products. The following chart below provides a general graphical overview.

Yellow	Green	Blue	Orange
Orange	Green	Brown	Green
Blue	Light Blue	Green	Grey
Orange	Light Green	Red	Lime Green
Purple	Dark Red	Green	Brown

THE TOMOTOMO IDENTITY
BASIC MANUAL

Packaging

For the packaging we have set aside two options in terms of materials and what the colour choice will be for the tomotomo logotype.

An option where there is a white packaging box, the tomotomo logotype colour will follow its original colour values.

Pantone: 199C
CMYK: C: 0, M: 85, Y: 100, K: 0

An option where there is a brown corrugated box packaging, the tomotomo logotype will be converted to the following colour value.

White: 100%

THE TOMOTOMO IDENTITY
BASIC MANUAL

Play catalogue

A catalogue was designed which showcases all the tomotomo toy products in a small and concise booklet. The identity of the brand is captured in the use of unique typography (Futura and Block typefaces), colours and images.

PLAY

tomotomo.

ROCKER
TRUNKEE
STACKER
CHOO-CHOO
FUTON RIDER
TOMODACHI

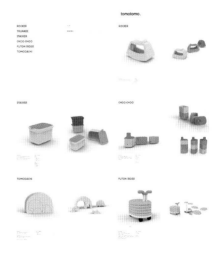

LED Field

A playground that captures the spirit of simple childlike play

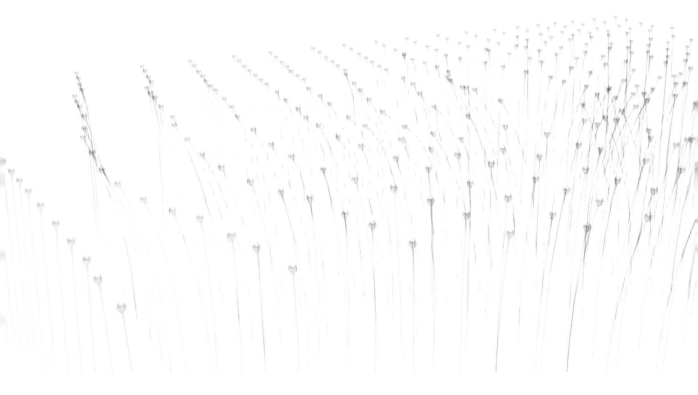

If a child runs, the LED Field sends a chasing light trail behind the child…
If the child stops to rest, the LEDs respond in kind by pausing at a distance…
If a child stamps his or her feet on the ground,
the Field emits a cascading wave of lights to amplify the action…
If the wind blows, the Field glows brighter or dimmer
according to the tilt of each stalk…
When it rains, the Field's lights flicker in sync to the rhythm of the raindrops…
If an adult runs in the Field and stamps his or her feet in the way that a child does,
the experience created may transport him or her back to a moment in their childhood…

Concept:

Created from an amalgamation of observations and idea sketches from other workshops conducted with children, the LED Field was designed to encapsulate the experience of joy that children exude on encountering situations of wonder and amazement and to distil it into an obvious interactive experience that any individual, young or old, is able to appreciate and respond to.

Can we filter or amplify the unrestrained joy of a child into a visually communicable quality or emotion?

1

2

3

1   Observation of children playing at a water fountain.
2   This technical design blueprint is for a single stalk that
     is designed to be mass-produced, making the LED
     Field concept highly scalable according to spatial needs.
3   Conceptual illustration of LED Field.

Prototyping as a Design Probe

Background:

Within the form-based practice of industrial and product design, the idea of a prototype generally is about the creation of a model or representation that is used as a visual and formal evaluation of how the product or object will look prior to actual production of the finalized design.

At the Centre we tend to view prototypes as more than just beautiful models or representations—here we treat the prototype itself as a tool for the creation of new designs. We use it to construct new ideas and as a probe to feed back users' responses and to find new directions. We also believe in putting simple prototyping tools into the hands of users and participants as a means of allowing them to express notions or ideas in ways that cannot be verbally articulated.

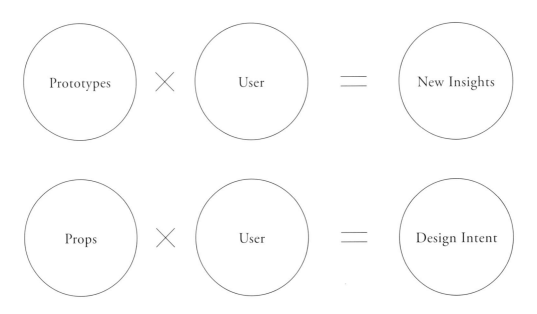

Opposite: One of the Centre's interns uses a model of a camera made by a child in order to gain insights into how children view the world around them.

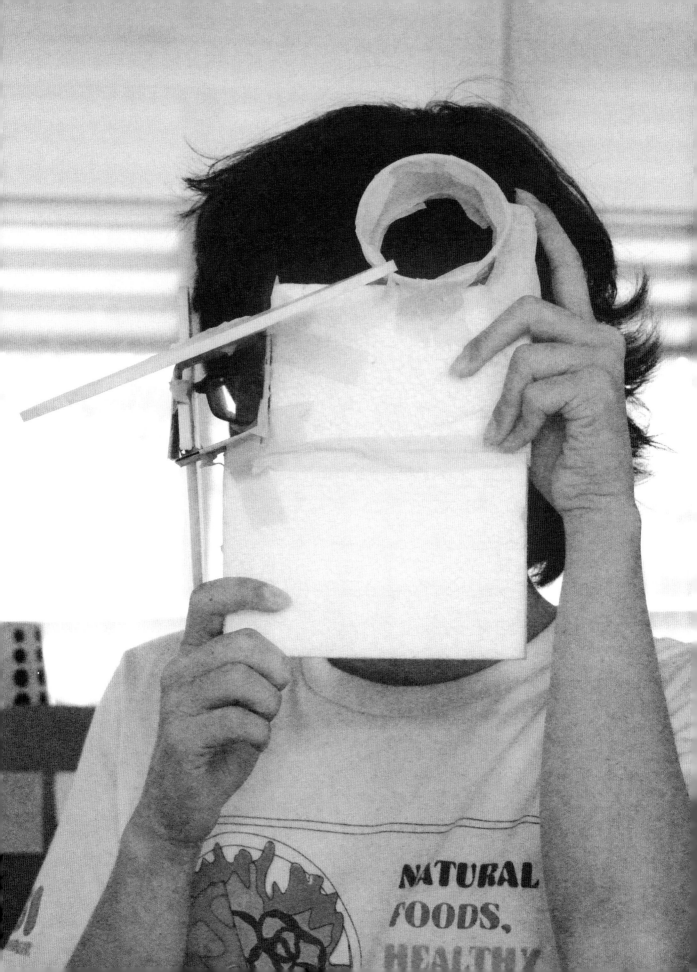

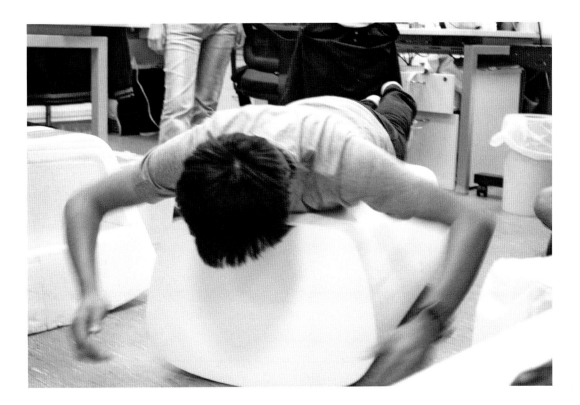

Insights:

> With all the toy prototypes created, the most striking observation the team noted was the fact that none of the children used the toys for their intended functions as prescribed by the Centre's designers. Instead, they often repurposed them for entirely new and novel play uses. We then realized that the toy designs or concepts that we came up with only formed half of the entire picture.
>
> When the prototypes were placed into the hands of children, something magical happened: the children did the unexpected, totally ignoring the original intent of the designers. This was a great revelation as it led to new insights, ideas and directions that we would have never been able to develop without going through this process of engagement with children.
>
> This planted the notion that as industrial or product designers, we were very much akin to costume or set makers. We would create the 'props' (prototypes) for the 'actors' (users) to get into character or set up the 'situations' (context) for things to take place. However, the 'story' has to be carried out and acted by the 'actors' themselves—very similar to the way a user completes a product by carrying out their own design intents.

Opposite: Kids from a local primary school playing with the same toy prototypes while the Centre's team conduct their own experiments. In this instance, we discovered that children play on the piece together at the same time, resulting in new play dynamics.
Above: The Centre's team conducting preliminary user experiments with rocking bench prototypes.

2 AUGMENTED SENSIBILITIES

On a trip to Osaka, Japan, organized by the Osaka Prefecture Government in 2006, we had the opportunity to visit some of the leading research institutes and companies that were working on robotics research. One of the research institutes we visited was founded and run by Professor Hiroshi Ishiguro, who was widely known as the man who created his own robotic clone.

During our meeting with him, the professor recalled an incident in which he was having a conversation with his assistant through his robotic clone. The professor was in his office while his assistant and the robotic clone were at a remote location. The assistant was talking to the clone and halfway through the conversation, the assistant reached out his hand and touched the robotic clone on the head; strangely, Professor Ishiguro was able to feel the touch physically even though he was not wired up in any way to receive this sense of touch.

This encounter with Professor Ishiguro sparked off a train of thought that there may exist another level of human consciousness which we are not aware of or attuned to which could possibly be unlocked through augmentation with robotic technology.

When developing these projects on robots, our goal was not to pursue technological sophistication but to use technology to uncover and activate our buried consciousness and emotions, and to discover and make new connections with ourselves.

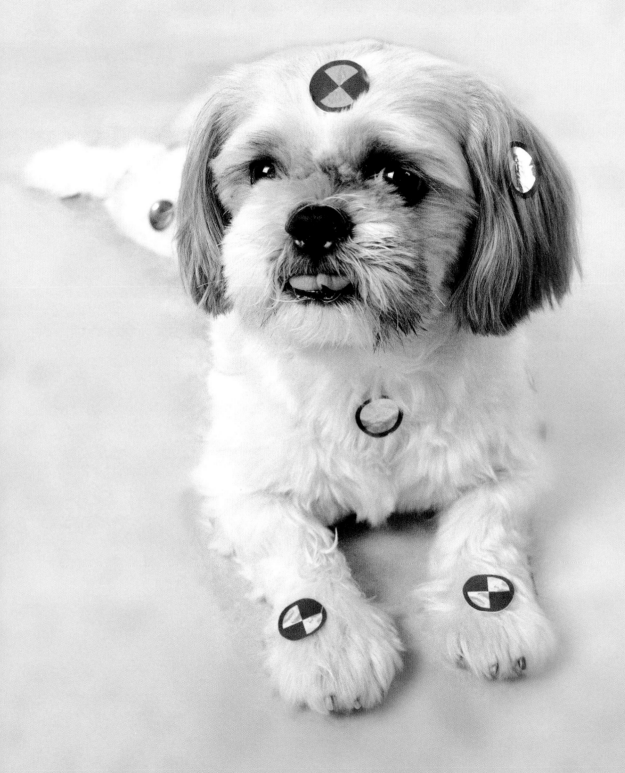

What is a Robot?

The current paradigm of what a robot is, is very much centred upon the humanoid form: how real and lifelike it can be, how intelligent and sophisticated the learning algorithms can get or how well robots can play sports such as football as a team.

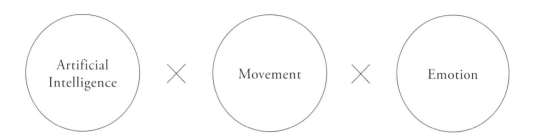

The current paradigm of what a robot is, is very much centred upon the humanoid form: how real and lifelike it can be, how intelligent and sophisticated the learning algorithms can get or how well robots can play sports such as football as a team.

    The Centre's robotic projects are interested in applying robotic technologies in different contexts and are framed to look beyond this dominant humanoid-centric obsession around which a lot of current robotics research is positioned.

    Our interest instead was in re-appropriating and re-looking at how these robots could be used in new and emerging social contexts, and in ways that would be more direct and sensible in daily living.

Opposite: Early trials of tagging a dog for digital captures during the Robot Dogs project

Robot Dogs

Cybernetic pet personalities

Background:

Advanced Media Inc. is an Osaka-based company that specializes in the creation, research and development of voice-recognition systems and speech technology. In a meeting with the Advanced Media Inc. representatives during our 2006 Osaka trip, they described a project they were working on in which a voice-recognition-equipped computer terminal was able to carry on a conversation with human users through asking questions and recording the users' responses.

These recorded responses would then be sorted and stored in a growing database to be used for replies in new conversations with future users, for example:

```
Terminal:   Where did you go for dinner last night?
  User 1:   I went to a restaurant in Roppongi.
Terminal:   What did you eat?
  User 1:   I had some sushi.
Terminal:   How was it?
  User 1:   It was delicious!
Terminal:   Would you recommend this restaurant to
            someone else?
  User 1:   Yes, definitely!
```

After this conversation, the computer terminal would then store the responses User 1 gave into its own database, to be used for a conversation with the next user:

```
Terminal:   Where did you go for dinner last night?
  User 2:   Oh, I went to an Italian place in Ginza.
Terminal:   I was at a restaurant in Roppongi.
            What did you eat in the Italian restaurant?
  User 2:   I had some pasta.
Terminal:   How was the food?
  User 2:   It was alright…
Terminal:   I had some sushi and it was delicious!
            I would definitely recommend this restaurant
            to you.
```

We observed that with a simple act of referencing and inserting collected data into conversations, the computer was able to project a sense of intelligence and personality.

Concept:

Imagine being able to transfer your dog's personality and behaviour into a database that would store and create a digital 'backup' of your dog's profile. Sensors would be installed in the rooms at your home or placed on your dog to capture and record its barks, movement patterns, reactions and responses to your commands and physical presence.

Then, on the demise of your dog, you could choose to transfer your dog's personality that has been stored in this database into a robotic life form to allow your dog to 'live' again. This robotic version of your dog would react, respond and behave in the same manner as your deceased dog by drawing from the database of information and behavioural patterns stored and collected during your dog's lifetime.

These behaviours and responses expressed by the new robotic dog might appear mechanical but would essentially retain the essence and familiarity of your late dog's character and personality.

Waiting for your dog to pass away just to be able to immortalize it as a robot seems like a rather morbid prospect… What if you could already download and adopt an existing dog's personality from another pet owner?

This idea opens up new domains of social and digital possibilities: What if dog personalities could be downloaded and exchanged like applications? What if the personality of a celebrity's dog could be downloaded into a robot dog from Apple's App Store? What if active communities of robot-pet owners started emerging around this phenomenon?

Dandella

Intuitive navigational device

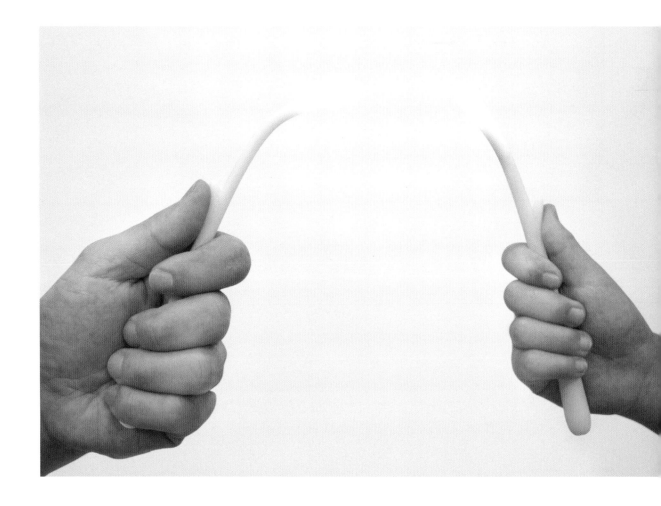

Dandella is a device that provides an intuitive approach to navigation by physically 'pointing' towards a designated direction, thus allowing users to instinctively find their way.

Inspired by the simple, universal gesture of pointing out directions, Dandella simplifies a complex global positioning device into the easily understood physical response of following the direction it points to.

How can the complex be made simple, intuitive and instinctive?

Dandella devices being used by a lost girl to find her father.

Is there a gestural, expressive form of communication...
a universal language that we are attuned to?

Background:

> We were looking for an intuitive and natural way to give and find directions besides the standard format and manner of referring to a physical map or any existing map software or device.

Concept:

> With Dandella we sought to create an object that would be understandable and usable without any need for complex learning. In the same way that it is instinctive to point out general directions if asked, Dandella is a navigational and way-finding device that taps into this particular strain of subconscious human action; an action that a child would understand instinctively.

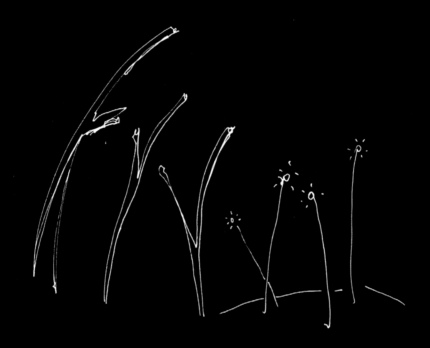

Initial sketch of the Dandella device

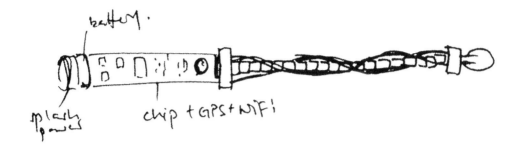

battery.

plash power

chip + GPS + WiFi

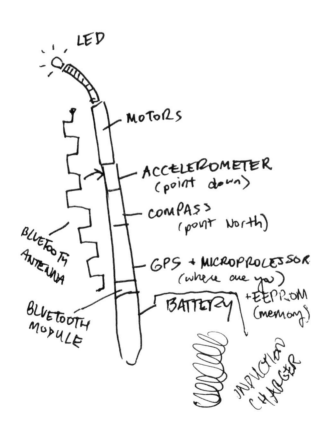

LED

MOTORS

ACCELEROMETER
(point down)

COMPASS
(point North)

GPS + MICROPROCESSOR
(where are you)

+ EEPROM
(memory)

BATTERY

BLUETOOTH ANTENNA

BLUETOOTH MODULE

INDUCTION CHARGER

This diagram was created by a research fellow we met in Osaka, who
broke down the inner workings of the Dandella device and illustrated the
possible engineering aspects on a napkin.

Roly Poly

Simulating presence

Concept:

When we inhabit the same house or room with another, we can often 'feel' or 'sense' the other person's presence through small nuances, for example, a light touch on our shoulders, the sound of rustling paper or the shuffling of feet.

The aim of Roly Poly was to capture this particular sense of 'presence' when both individuals no longer inhabit the same space. Connected through the Internet, both Roly Poly devices are mirrors of each other.

If you move one of the two devices, the very same movement will be echoed in the other: a slight nudge or a hard push will be equally expressed—this in turn opens up an exclusive interpersonal communication channel between individuals located in two different locations and reintroduces the idea of 'presence' despite the distance.

The Roly Poly devices being demonstrated during SIGGRAPH 2011 in Vancouver, Canada.

Insights:

Through observations of people interacting and using Roly Poly during various exhibitions and demonstrations, we realized an important and key insight for the Centre: a product, more often than not, is completed and 'finished' by the user themselves and their impressions and perceptions of it. Perhaps it was about a product expressing simple visual cues or containing certain triggers that would allow a user to project his or her expectations onto the product.

By allowing and accommodating the projection of these ideas and expectations, a product transcends itself by becoming a platform: the finishing and completion of a product is then not done by designers but by users.

Touch Hear

An intuitive text-recognition dictionary

What if I could understand the meaning of a word or know the pronunciation of a French expression by simply brushing the surface of a page with my fingertips?

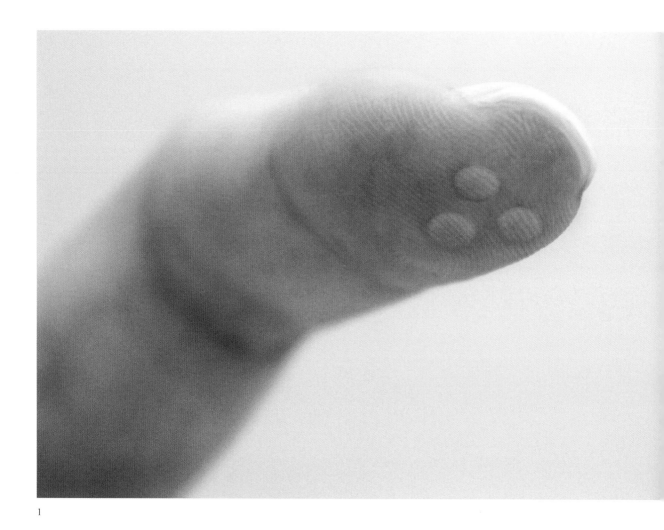

1

1   Body Area Network Transmitter: Finger Implant with character-recognition system.
2   Using Touch Hear and a word-recognition system while reading.
3   Body Area Network Receiver: Ear Receiver Module and the Text-to-Speech System.

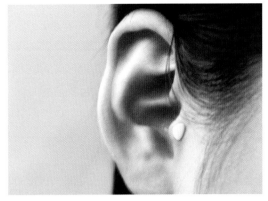

2 3

Background:

> This project was inspired by situations that happen often while reading: we come across familiar words that we never quite seem to know the precise meaning of or encounter expressions in a foreign tongue for which we do not always know the correct pronunciation...
>
> Touch Hear aims to make accessing such information and knowledge seamless and non-disruptive to our reading experiences.

Concept:

> Conceived as a text- and language-recognition dictionary implanted into the human body—at the fingertips and the ear through nanotechnology—the ubiquitous nature of the Touch Hear device would allow an individual to obtain (or hear through an audio implant) information from a database of native and foreign word pronunciations, meanings and terminologies without interrupting their flow of reading.

Insights:

> As we developed this project, we considered the various ways and forms in which the device could exist: as a digital pen scanner, an external device to fit over your hand and an attachment onto the fingernails.
>
> Through these iterations, we eventually determined that for Touch Hear to be truly as ubiquitous and seamless as we envisioned it, it had to fit so well that it would be invisible, or be designed to exist as a component of the human body.
>
> Although this made the project's concept seem almost science fiction-like, we felt that this was the fitting approach to take. The idea of body implants may seem invasive or repulsive, but if we examine our history, we will notice that the act of body modification is essentially a large part of many civilizations; the installation of the device would simply be part of a behavioural and cultural response that is actually quite natural and innate to us.

Papa Bear

Bridging the gap between the genius and non-genius

Background:

Papa Bear was inspired by an article about a two-year-old child who learnt to read independently after being read to by her father for a few weeks. We were wondering how this child was able to connect the sounds spoken by her father to the words shown on the page—perhaps she was able to 'crack the code' of reading?

 This led us to consider if the difference between a genius and a normal child might depend on the genius's innate ability to make the connections between the words on a page and the voice of the parent. A possible difference between the genius and a normal child might be that one was able to make the word-to-voice connections naturally while the latter was unable to do so.

 If, then, we could create and provide a tool that would enable the normal child to bridge this gap, would the normal child be able to effectively reach the level of a genius?

Concept:

Papa Bear is a concept for a physical book that uses hidden technology to enable a child to make the right connections between what they would see (the words on a page) and hear (a parent reading those words).

Insights:

During development, we intuitively knew that the experience of being read a bedtime story—the setting and parent-to-child interaction—was crucial to the concept, and insisted that it had to be executed without disrupting or taking away this experience.

 When Papa Bear was developed, tablet devices were not as prominent as they currently are. The first iteration of the concept was a book with hidden voice-recognition technology that would enable the words on a page to light up in response to a person's reading.

 The introduction of the iPad and the subsequent range of tablet devices that emerged in the market gave us the realization that a tablet might actually be the perfect platform for re-implementing the Papa Bear concept.

 An application for a tablet would function in very much the same way that a physical book would, as the setting, experience and interaction would not be affected at all.

1

1 The first iteration of the Papa Bear concept
   was based on a book format.
2 The second iteration of the concept was
   designed as an application for the iPad.

2

3 SENSIBILITIES AND LIMITATIONS

Sensibilities and Limitations was a design research study conducted by the Centre that explored the possibilities for the Silver (elderly) Industry from a design perspective. Two workshops, Sensibilities and Limitations I and II, each addressed a different scope of active aging. This chapter is a comprehensive report and summary that compiles the processes, tools and structures of the workshops and is intended to be a guide and reference for readers who are looking into conducting their own workshops.

Sensibilities and Limitations Workshop I: The Elderly and Info-Communications Technology

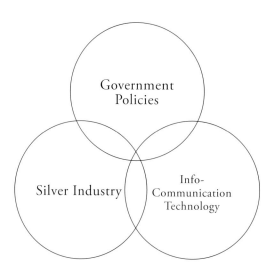

Background:

Sensibilities and Limitations I focused on the theme of info-communications and the Silver Industry by investigating how the elderly engage with technology in their daily lives and activities.

     The workshop's aim was to challenge the divide that existed between the elderly and digital technology and to understand how they might make use of technology to communicate, carry out daily routines and facilitate lifelong learning for themselves.

     To raise awareness for the Silver Industry in the info-communications sector, key government stakeholders and commercial partners were invited to participate in a series of discussions geared towards the development of innovative products, services and spaces that would encourage independent living for the elderly.

     The design outcomes that were developed emphasized being sensitive towards the entire well-being of the elderly, acting as examples of inclusive design rather than obtrusive design. The following is a summary of the first workshop with some of the project outcomes detailed.

Workshop Documentation

Part 1:
The Elderly and
Info-Communications Technology

25th — 27th February 2008

Conducted by the Design Incubation Centre
Supported by the Council for Third Age (C3A)

Workshop Context

The Silver Industry no longer consists of elderly consumers who are stereotypically dependent and conservative. On the contrary, there is an emerging resource pool of active, experienced and talented seniors.

These Third Age seniors, though open-minded and healthy in spirit, will inevitably experience gradual changes to their physical health and mobility. Our initial research has shown that most products and services are not designed to address the limitations of the elderly, and ad hoc adaptations are usually made to existing products to overcome these limitations.

With an elderly consumer group becoming more significant, it is important to consider and cater to their physical abilities and psychological expectations when we design for them.

Workshop Participants

The workshop was a good platform that encouraged the cross-pollination of disciplines, ideas and initiatives between the four categories of multi-disciplinary participants and speakers:

1 **The Government:**
   Ministry of Community Development, Youth and Sports (MCYS) and The Council for Third Age

2 **Commercial Info-communications:**
   Philips Design and The A*Star Institute for Infocomm Research

3 **The Silver Industry:**
   Retired & Senior Volunteer Programme (RSVP)

4 **Design and Education:**
   Staff and student designers from The National University of Singapore's Faculty of Engineering, Faculty of Industrial Design and Design Exchange, a Singapore-based design consultancy

Workshop Strategy

The strategy for the workshop sought to combine research on the Silver Industry with information on info-communications technologies to search for new design needs and opportunities.

To obtain a holistic overview on the workshop topic of the elderly and info-communications, participants were split into three groups looking into different themes based on active schemes that were being implemented by the government, namely:

1 **Social Communication**
2 **Independent Living**
3 **Lifelong Learning**

The observational studies conducted during the workshop focused on interaction with the elderly to learn about their lifestyle, needs and difficulties.

Field visits to info-communications showrooms were also included to educate and inform the workshop participants on current and future technology needs.

Participants Diagram

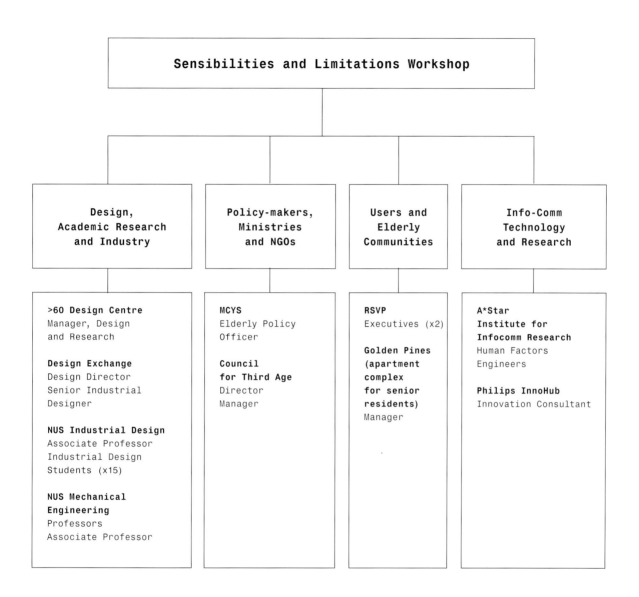

Sensibilities and Limitations Workshop

Design, Academic Research and Industry

>60 Design Centre
Manager, Design and Research

Design Exchange
Design Director
Senior Industrial Designer

NUS Industrial Design
Associate Professor
Industrial Design Students (x15)

NUS Mechanical Engineering
Professors
Associate Professor

Policy-makers, Ministries and NGOs

MCYS
Elderly Policy Officer

Council for Third Age
Director
Manager

Users and Elderly Communities

RSVP
Executives (x2)

Golden Pines (apartment complex for senior residents)
Manager

Info-Comm Technology and Research

A*Star
Institute for Infocomm Research
Human Factors Engineers

Philips InnoHub
Innovation Consultant

Workshop Process

The Design Incubation Centre's workshop process is always tailored to suit the context and objectives of each workshop through a combination and usage of research methods and design tools.

Of the five phases in the entire process, the participants are involved in four — from the 'Gathering Insights' to the 'Proof' phase, while the 'Pre-research' phase is conducted by the Centre's team prior to the workshop's commencement.

The tools used for observation, organization, analysis and idea-generation that were selected for use in this workshop are elaborated in the Process Diagram opposite, and also in the Workshop Toolbox section.

Sensibilities and Limitations Workshop I started by collecting profiles of the participants' parents. This was integral to identifying the social spectrum of the elderly for whom we were designing. The workshop participants then observed the elderly from afar and personally interacted with and interviewed them in their living spaces and learning environments.

After sufficient field observations were gathered, the groups then returned to the workshop studio to consolidate and analyze their findings to gain useful design insights. These design insights were then transformed through the usage of organization and ideation tools to create innovative universal design solutions.

Process Diagram

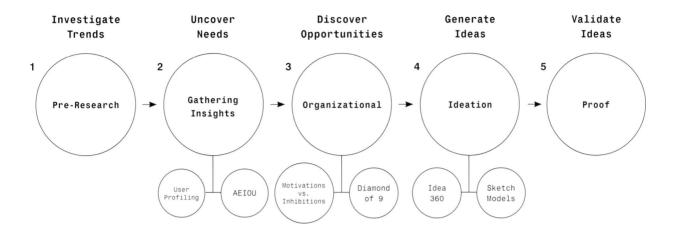

Investigate Trends	Uncover Needs	Discover Opportunities	Generate Ideas	Validate Ideas
1 Pre-Research	2 Gathering Insights	3 Organizational	4 Ideation	5 Proof
	User Profiling / AEIOU	Motivations vs. Inhibitions / Diamond of 9	Idea 360 / Sketch Models	

1 Pre-Research

a Exhibition Visit:
The Centre's team visited partners in the Sicex '08 conference and exhibition to understand their views on the workshop topic.

b Literature Review and Online Search:
Used to build background knowledge on the workshop's topic.

2 Gathering Insights

a User Profiling:
Collection of detailed demographics about the users to understand common and upcoming trends relevant to them.

b AEIOU (Activities, Environment, Interactions, Objects, Users):
We expanded our scope of observation to look beyond the most direct subjects we would encounter.

3 Organizational

a Motivations vs. Inhibitions:
The identification of push and pull factors behind the activities the users do or do not carry out.

b Diamond of 9:
Used to strategically rate the push and pull factors in a hierarchy as a method of evaluation.

4 Ideation

a Idea 360:
An ideation method based on the circulation of concepts. Sitting in a circle or around a table, each individual is given a drawing board. They are encouraged to sketch an idea on the board's centre, and then to circulate it by passing to the person on their right.

5 Proof of Concepts

a Sketch Models:
Simple prototypes are then created to illustrate and test ideas within an allocated short time frame.

For information on the complete Workshop Toolbox, please refer to page 70.

Summary of Workshop Events

Day 1:
Introduction and
Gathering Insights

Introductory Talk:

Sensibilities and Limitations Workshop I commenced with an introductory talk covering the purpose, rationale and desired outcomes as well as an overview presentation to assign the various participants into their groups and themes.

Insight Gathering:

The insight-gathering method 'AEIOU' was also introduced to the participants during the presentation.

Field Visit:

Next, field visits were made to several government agency partners to allow them to introduce pertinent issues and future plans to the participants to enable them to gain a better grasp of the overall subject matter and context. The participants then finally separated into their groups to head off to the assigned locations to conduct observational studies on the elderly in various learning and living environments.

Day 2:
Lectures, Visits and the
Organizational Phase

Design & Technologies Introduction:

The second day of the workshop began with a presentation on the 'Future of Aging' and a design lecture on 'Inclusive Design', delivered by the Head of Industrial Design. The 'Seven Principles of Universal Design' were also introduced to the participants. Next, a visit to a commercial info-communications partner, A*Star, was conducted where the researchers there presented new innovations and technologies.

Observation Analysis and Idea Generation:

Participants also began the Organizational phase by sorting and ranking various photos and insights with the 'Motivations vs. Inhibitions' and 'Diamond of 9' tools. The key insights were then selected and the ideation process began with the usage of the 'Idea 360' method. At all times, the Centre's team was on hand to guide, assist and facilitate the sessions.

Day 3:
Proof of Concepts and
Presentations

Post-Workshop Activity
carried out by the
Design Incubation Centre:

Idea Refinement:

The last day of Sensibilities and
Limitations Workshop I started
with the selection and refinement
of the participants' ideas
developed during the previous
day. Simple prototypes were
created and large posters drawn
out to aid in the illustration of
the refined concepts.

Further Review and Refinement of
Selected Concepts:

The team at the Design Incubation
Centre spent 1–2 months
consolidating the insights and
ideas that were generated during
the workshop by the participants.
Later, these insights were
reviewed and refined into
concrete concepts.

Final Presentation:

The participant groups then
delivered a final presentation:
observations, insights and
concepts were presented with
conclusive comments being given
at the end by the Centre's
team and representatives from
the Council for Third Age. The
workshop then concluded with
a feedback session to gather
participant suggestions.

Key insights and observations
with potential were then gathered
by the Centre and taken back for
further design development.

Communication of Outcomes:

A selection of concepts were
communicated in the form of a
print document and published
on the Design Incubation Centre's
website.

Workshop Toolbox

Developed and adapted by
Cheong Yian Ling

This toolbox was accumulated from readings and personal participation in several design thinking workshops. Each time, after learning a new tool and noting down its benefits and limitations, I would modify them slightly to fit my subsequent workshops.

Tools (T) may come in the form of a framework, template or even a principle.

Methods (M) refer to how these tools can be applied. Designing purposeful and thoughtful methods to an effective tool is key to reaping insightful results in the design process.

OBSERVE

Memory Sketch
T — To illustrate past experiences from memory in physical sketches.
M — Recall personal history and sketch memorable or important moments which are related to the design topic. Instead of taking photos, trace your daily routine/experiences and sketch them in detail on paper.

Interview
T — Elicit information directly from the users.
M — Spend some time building up a relationship with user. Ask open-ended questions to share freely. Prepare no questions, but allow user to guide and start telling stories related to the context. During a workshop, participants can interview each other to create profiles.

AEIOU
T — Activity, Environment, Interaction, Object, User.
A framework to look at the bigger and complete picture.
M — Through photo taking, make observations of the target users using AEIOU framework. Hold discussions guided by the framework.

100 photos
T — Collect in-depth information using 100 photos.
M — Take 100 photos regarding a vaguely defined topic, open to wide interpretation. Prepare a variety of 100 photos, print them, and allow users to sort and rank them.

ANALYSE

Needs, wants, barriers and limitations
T — Uncover each of the above and group them accordingly in hierarchy.
M — Annotate photos collected from Observe and categorize them in four segments. From interviews, analyze the mental models of users according to their needs, wants, barriers and limitations. If possible, sort them further in their four segments.

Five models
from Prof. Naohito Okude's workshop
T — Make sense out of the AEIOU framework by constructing the five models.
M — Activity, Environment, Interaction, Object, User. Sketch these models on large pieces of paper to study the dynamics among the models.

Idea critic
from Future Lab workshop

T — Designing backwards, starting from a solution. Useful for tight design spaces which are already saturated with plenty of solutions.

M — Present a variety of design solutions which are published and discuss their pros and cons. If possible, try the solutions first-hand and evaluate experiences.

Motivations and challenges

T — Useful when the topic requires users to accept something new.

M — Studying the photos, sketches and interview notes, mine the motivations and challenges faced by the users. Make sense within these two broad groups and group the insights into sub-categories.

BRAINSTORM

What if

T — Asking the right question so as to direct the right solution.

M — With all analysis clearly displayed, formulate questions which suggest a design opportunity/direction, starting each question with, 'What if…'. Try to keep questions general but thought-provoking.

Philosophy and vision
from Prof. Naohito Okude's workshop

T — To cast a vision far into the future, assuming all things are possible.

M — Imagine you are the inventor of an invention which is the most amazing to date. What do you think could have been the philosophy and vision behind it? Now you are an inventor of objects for the future, what will be your philosophy and vision? Write down users' aspirations for the future, expecting the unexpected.

Idea 360

T — Some individual time to generate ideas and build on one another's thought process

M — Give out drawing boards to every individual and sit them in a circle. Encourage everyone to sketch an idea on the centre of the board. Once done, pass your board to the person on your right and work on that idea or simply sketch a new one.

Random word match

T — Allowing the chemistry of words and human imagination to generate some unexpected ideas. Useful for topics which are not trying to solve any problems.

M — Write down as many words as possible which are directly or indirectly related to the topic. Randomly pick 2 to 3 words, string them together and make meaning through ideas.

Claystorming
from Prof. Naohito Okude's workshop

T — Create clay sculptures to represent ideas.

M — With a design direction in place, mould a lump of clay to illustrate an idea you have in mind. As one is moulding the clay, it is easy to get inspired and start moulding more details which are thought of through sculpting.

REFINE

Why and why not

T — Repeated questioning to ensure idea is thoroughly justified.

M — Asking a series of 'why' questions from different perspectives can help us think deeply about an idea. After deconstructing the idea using 'why' questions, rebuild the idea using 'why not' solutions.

Blueprints

T — Mapping out all touchpoints and flow of information in a complex interaction. Useful for service or system design.

M — By sketching a blueprint of all interactions which take place on a large piece of paper, we can study the situation by looking for loopholes or opportunities for value-adding to the idea.

Storyboards

T — Refining the idea by going through a possible scenario from beginning to end.

M — Drawing a storyboard/comic strip of the scenario helps to ensure that the idea is applicable throughout the process flow from need to use. It may reveal events whereby we need to remove, add or change features of the original idea.

Mid-term checkup

T — Consulting users to check usefulness of ideas.

M — It is never too early to involve users in the design process. Even with a rough idea, the users, being experts in their own field, may be able to provide insights to propel the idea forward. This stage is timely to check if the users find the concepts useful and if they can imagine themselves using them in the future.

PROTOTYPE

Sketch prototype

T — Rough prototype to demonstrate idea and simulate the use scenario.

M — Using ready materials and other craft materials, make quick mock-ups to illustrate the concept. Aesthetics is not entirely important at this stage, but try to make the prototype representative enough to test and prove certain parts

of the concepts. Make several prototypes to allow users to make comparisons. Bring it out for testing with target users.

Hyperlink prototype

T — Fast and easy to create digital interfaces for testing.

M — Using Powerpoint or other digital sketch tools, we can build hard-coded interfaces to allow users to get a taste of the designed experience. At this stage, investing into detailed software programming might involve too much effort and time.

Toolbox Acknowledgements

Certain tools used in the toolbox
were adapted from the following
sources:

100 photos
    RSA workshop

AEIOU
    Doblin

Five models
    Prof. Naohito Okude

Idea critic
    Future Lab

Claystorming
    Prof. Naohito Okude

Idea 360
    Source unknown

Philosophy and vision
    Prof. Naohito Okude

Random word match
    Atelier HOKO

What if
    IDEO

Blueprints
    This is Service Design Thinking
    by Marc Stickdorn and Jakob
    Schneider (2012)

Why and why not
    IDEO

Hyperlink prototype
    *Prototyping: A Practitioner's
    Guide* by Todd Zaki Warfel (2009)

Workshop Outcomes

Overview:

The use of familiar analogue archetypes often acts as a trigger that effectively breaks down the entry barriers of technology. The choice of utilizing everyday objects and tying a non-digital function to an existing digital one was very much an intuitive reaction to the key theme identified in Sensibilities and Limitations Workshop I.

The prototypes and concepts shown are intended to be 'bridging devices' that seek to create familiar situations that the elderly can instinctively recognize and react to.

For example, Pen and Paper repurposes a letter by merging the analogue and tactile manner of writing on a sheet of paper with the function of emailing. Digital functions often hide behind a graphic user interface that is foreign to an elderly person. In this instance, the interface disappears and becomes an inherent part of the tool and its function.

Digital Magnifier

Concept:

The Digital Magnifier creates a physical interface between an elderly user and technology by having a single function, the enlargement of onscreen items and information.

Connected through a USB port, the software that comes with the Magnifier refocuses portions of the computer screen that it scans over, thus offering instantaneous, sharp image enlargements to assist in the viewing of small onscreen content.

The usage of the Digital Magnifier in a physically familiar manner echoes the act of using an actual magnifying glass, hence nurturing the usage of technology in an intuitive way that reduces the complexity required to operate and view digital information.

Pen and Paper

Observations:

We observed that the elderly experienced difficulty in finding the keys on the keyboard. They also exhibited difficulty in typing out an email message and were observed expressing uncertainty as to whether emails sent were received.

Insights:

Many elderly folk who are not English-language-educated find it difficult to understand the computer's interface. The letter arrangement of the keys on the keyboard often does not make any sense to the elderly and they found the idea of writing a letter by hand much quicker than typing out an email message.

Concept:

Electronic mail has replaced the customized and heartwarming quality of handwritten letters and notes. Pen and Paper requires a user to place a sheet of paper onto a pressure-sensitive surface, which projects a simple graphic template. With an ordinary pen or pencil, any text written on the paper shows up correspondingly onscreen. After the writing is done, the elderly user can simply send out the letter as an email without incurring mail costs.

Net Phone

Observations:

There is a lack of suitable instant-messaging programs available that are easy enough for the elderly to use. Often, their children will need to set up the entire process for them before the conferencing and messaging functions can be fully utilized.

Insights:

Most Internet conferencing and messaging programs involve a complex process: downloading, un-compressing, acknowledgement of terms and registration before the program finally loads. The complexity of using software to make a call through the Internet is still a foreign concept for most elderly folk, and the layered steps are confusing.

Concept:

The Net Phone is designed to allow elderly users to make free Internet calls without hassle while retaining the familiarity of holding a telephone receiver and enjoying a conversation for hours.

Upon plugging in, the Net Phone automatically installs and integrates itself with existing conferencing and messaging software and places the user online without fuss. By dialling the analogue numbers on the Phone, the user is able to bypass the complex functions involved through a digital interface.

Selection Knob Button

Observations:

In a class that taught the elderly how to use the Internet, the team observed that they: (1) pointed at the screen even though they knew that onscreen items cannot be selected by 'touching'; (2) wrote down instructions meticulously in notebooks; (3) often closed and restarted a program whenever a pop-up box appeared; and (4) used a magnifying glass to enlarge and see onscreen items clearly.

Insights:

Digital interfaces are not intuitive and the sequential 'steps' involved make doing a simple task like emailing tedious and daunting. The folder within folder structure and the layering of information is confusing for the elderly.

Concept:

For functions (such as emailing or Internet browsing) that require the use of a program, a physical selection knob can be plugged in to scroll through and select the required program, functioning like the tuning dial on a radio.

The interference and layering caused by the presence of a complex user interface and from other applications are removed, allowing one object or program to be shown clearly for selection.

Concierge Helpline

Observations:

Emergency pull-cords in studio apartments for the elderly are hardly used at all. We observed that the reason for this might be to avoid the embarrassment that the elderly user might face if the proportion of aid received exceeds the amount of help they really need.

Insights:

A call-for-help service could be implemented to cater to different degrees of emergencies and needs. There is a need to have a person at the end of the line to determine the urgency and nature of the aid required.

Concept:

This service concept is modelled after concierge services and telephone helplines where a person is available by phone as a single point of contact to provide a large range of personalized services to the elderly user. The potential high cost of employing dedicated helpline personnel can be mediated through the outsourcing of manpower to more cost-efficient countries and economies, and by tapping into existing services provided through the Internet.

Payment Dongle

Observations:

When making payments, there is a general sense of apprehension among the elderly regarding hidden surcharges that may be incurred without their knowledge. However, we noted that they are receptive towards the idea of paying hourly rates at an Internet service centre and to the usage of pre-paid mobile phone cards as they have better control over the amount of money that will be spent.

Insights:

Time-based and hourly-rated services need to be clear and transparent as to when the charging would begin, how and when the charging can be stopped and the cost of the rate in order to gain the elderly user's confidence in the services.

Concept:

The Payment Dongle is an external device that is activated by plugging in to existing digital devices such as mobile and smart phones, laptops and desktops to enable the usage of time-based services.

When connected, the prepaid amount contained within the card, as well as the usage time left, will be shown on the Dongle's interface. Unplugging the Dongle will disconnect the service used immediately and reflect the updated amount and usage time left accordingly.

Sensibilities and Limitations Workshop II: The Elderly and Employment

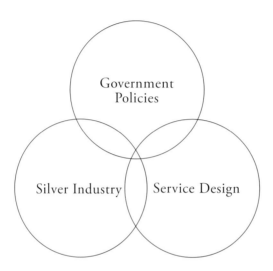

Background:

Sensibilities and Limitations Workshop II aimed at examining the Silver Industry employment situation within our existing workforce through the lens of the design process.

An extension of Sensibilities and Limitations I, the second workshop was triggered by an observation of elderly cleaners forming long queues to clock out of their workday.

This felt like a waste of these workers' time and seemed to suggest that there was insufficient thought and consideration given to the workplace and lifestyle needs of a silver workforce.

The heart of the second workshop can be said to lie in the idea of repurposing and redesigning existing workplace situations to adopt a more considered approach towards elderly workers and proposed the creation of a new employment model that might redeploy them in a more efficient and sympathetic manner.

SENSIBILITIES + LIMITATIONS WORKSHOP II
SILVER TALENTS
知觉＋局限工作坊
银发人才

A DESIGN WORKSHOP FOR THE SILVER WORKING COMMUNITY
银发族与职业设计工作坊

PRESENTED BY
THE DESIGN INCUBATION CENTRE

FRIDAY, 26 SEPTEMBER 2008
9:00 AM — 6:00 PM

NATIONAL UNIVERSITY OF SINGAPORE
DEPARTMENT OF ARCHITECTURE
SCHOOL OF DESIGN & ENVIRONMENT BLOCK 1
LEVEL 2, STAFF LOUNGE

As the workforce in Singapore continues to age, challenges to the economy and employment structure are inevitable. Potential employers seek a company of competent employees while silver workers desire to continue contributing to the economy. Their desire to work and talents are often undervalued, resulting in uncertainty of their retirement careers.

This workshop aims to investigate on the silver working community, discovering this pool of silver talents and designing new business services to help them work and age actively with a sense of satisfaction. Innovative service designs can play a part in retaining, retraining and recruiting the elderly into the workforce.

新加坡的劳动阶层日渐趋向老化，社会的经济与就业结构难免会受到影响。雇主需要寻找能干的员工，银发族也渴望持续留在或回返工作岗位为社会做出贡献。但是，因为年纪的增长，雇主往往会低估他们的工作能力。

我们的工作坊正为银发族调查探索，发觉他们的潜能并设计新的工作机会，让他们重新出发改变人生。创新的服务设计希望可以协助他们赶上社会步伐，对新的工作怀有信心及热忱。

DIC Design Incubation Centre **NUS**

The Design Incubation Centre is a design research laboratory which investigates and develops new design tools to find new possibilities for the practice of design. This is done through projects that analyze the emerging and evolving human needs, technology and social trends. The Design Incubation Centre is part of the Department of Architecture at the School of Design and Environment in the National University of Singapore.

www.designincubationcentre.com
www.arch.nus.edu.sg

Workshop Process

Working together with participants from several government stakeholders that have an interest in mobilizing an active silver workforce, the Centre's team initiated the second workshop aimed at exploring potential possibilities in retaining, retraining and recruiting more elderly people into the silver workforce sector.

Through an interaction and interview session with different senior citizens with different skill profiles, the workshop participants began ideating and mapping out preliminary service blueprints in order to understand the motivations and limitations of the elderly.

Blueprints and concepts that held potential for expansion were then taken back by the Centre's team to be refined into viable concepts for implementation.

Creative Tools:

Each participant was given a workshop journal that was filled with descriptions of open-ended creative tools to aid them in collecting first-hand insights from the elderly.

Profiling:

Past work experiences, current job statuses and future plans shared by the elderly enabled the workshop participants to build user profiles that they could create ideas for.

Sharing:

Workshop participants were formed into groups to share and discuss the various profiles of the elderly that they encountered to reveal possible design opportunities.

Profile Charts:

Specific user information was collected from the various user profiles and plotted into a Profile Chart. This Chart mapped out the various factors that motivated or affected the elderly users and were condensed into evocative keywords that would act as points of inspiration.

Ideation:

A rich pool of creative ideas and concepts were developed through the asking and proposal of 'what if' questions and scenarios by the workshop participants to challenge and address the stereotype of elderly workers.

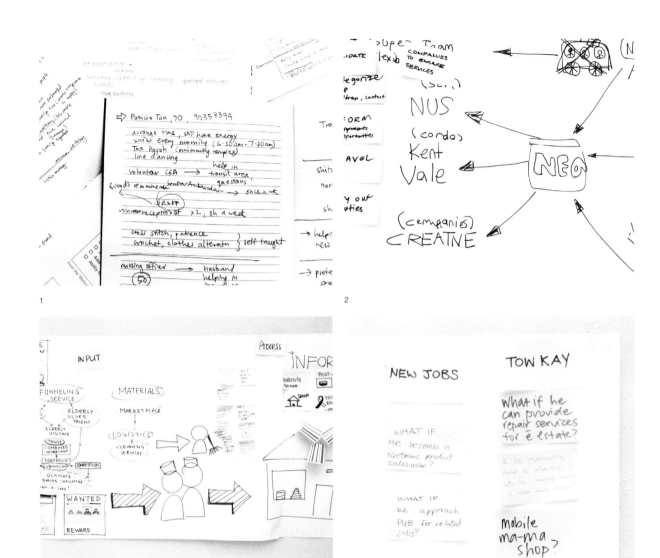

1 User profile from participant's handbook.
2 Environmental agency service blueprint diagram.
3 Medical service blueprint diagram.
4 'What if' questions.

Workshop Outcome:

The Service Blueprint
for Environmental Agencies

Silver Team   **1** Each Silver Team is made up of seniors who have accumulated years of
experience in their field of work. They form an all-round team, providing
transport and quality environmental maintenance services.

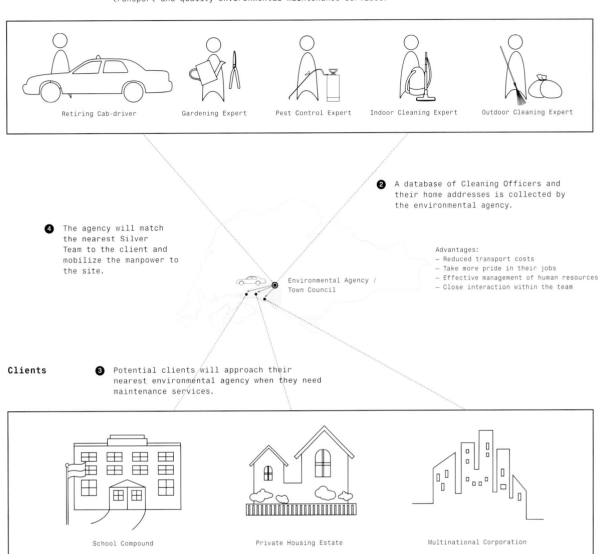

Retiring Cab-driver   Gardening Expert   Pest Control Expert   Indoor Cleaning Expert   Outdoor Cleaning Expert

2 A database of Cleaning Officers and
their home addresses is collected by
the environmental agency.

4 The agency will match
the nearest Silver
Team to the client and
mobilize the manpower to
the site.

Environmental Agency /
Town Council

Advantages:
— Reduced transport costs
— Take more pride in their jobs
— Effective management of human resources
— Close interaction within the team

Clients   **3** Potential clients will approach their
nearest environmental agency when they need
maintenance services.

School Compound   Private Housing Estate   Multinational Corporation

The diagram illustrates a concept for a sympathetic deployment system
for a silver workforce. It breaks down the possible ways in which silver
employees can be employed in work locations closer to their homes to
reduce the commuting cost and time that will be spent.

The reduction of commuting cost and time translates indirectly, over a
period of time, into more hours and disposable income that can be spent
on leisure and lifestyle activities, thus enriching their aging years
through both work and play.

4 INITIATIVES, PLATFORMS AND FELLOWSHIPS

It has been said that luck only happens to those who are ready for it. In the spirit of that saying, many of the Centre's projects and workshops are self-initiated. On the one hand, they serve as platforms for our research and investigation. On the other, they prepare us to be ready when opportunities arise.

Many of these self-initiated projects are investigative and experimental in nature. The results of these investigations often provide a new wealth of insights and possibilities. Acting on these possibilities, some of these projects are transformed into new platforms onto which future projects could be built.

For example, the d.lab brand started as an experimental workshop which evolved into a brand that the students could tap into, and also acted as a vehicle for attracting collaborations. Lessons learnt from the Centre's commercial activities are always brought back to the teaching fold through new projects framed around the d.lab brand.

Although the Centre is not a commercial entity, we see that design is only completed when the ideas are successfully implemented and the desired impact has been achieved. As such, when we are developing new projects, we are also finding new ways in which the ideas behind them can be successfully implemented, commercialized and used repeatedly.

This outlook has also changed the way we measure and assess the projects developed through teaching. More recently, both the students and the faculty have been looking at their studio projects not as mere assignments necessary for completing the course work, but as projects which, when implemented, could make a real impact, be it for one person or a million people.

At the same time, we are always improvising and creating new schemes on the fly to support projects that are interesting for the Centre and also to support students and staff who have shown talent or inclinations for a particular area of investigation.

Being from a small country with a small manufacturing base and consumer market, we have learnt to adopt the view of 'the world as both our manufacturing backyard and our market'. This has led us to initiate projects with various companies both abroad and within Singapore. This is not done with the intent of commercial gain but as lessons in understanding how we can engage these companies with new value propositions.

The Centre is an opportunistic animal. It is constantly evaluating its position and changing its direction whenever new information and new opportunities arise.

Objects and Accessories Workshop

Background:

Objects and Accessories was a workshop that set the stage for d.lab as it eventually transformed into a vehicle with commercially viable weight and value. Essentially a materials exploration workshop, it sought new possibilities in creating a product collection that would exploit the emotive and tactile qualities of the Corian® material.

1   A field visit to the OSA fabrication factory to observe different production methods used by the workers in their manufacturing processes. The craftsmen demonstrated how to cut Corian® pieces to ensure a perfect and seamless bond between two surfaces.

2   Material exploration during the workshop. Corian® is very versatile and can be joined, thermoformed to shapes, and laser-etched with patterns on its surface.

3   The material is heated up to temperatures between 140°C and 160°C before being formed around wooden jigs.

4–8   Prototypes from the workshop were made from the first-hand experimentation with Corian® by the participants. As the inherent qualities of Corian® were explored through different manufacturing processes, the functionality and product applications of each aesthetic possibility were also considered. This process eventually led to a distinct sensitivity to the material and each object's function in our final designs.

1

2

3

4

5

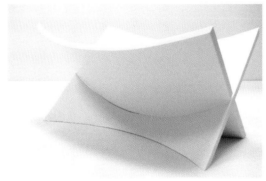

6

7

8

d.lab

l block - no 001 / 100

d.lab *Objects around the tablescape*

d.lab is about design at its most elemental level: the object's material, form, proportion and arrangement, and the relationship that exists between the object and its background.

Background:

The intention from the Objects and Accessories Workshop was always to develop and produce a collection of products with which we could eventually mount an exhibition. However, the team did not want the entire initiative to be a one-off event that would end with the exhibition and decided to create a commercial entity out of this endeavour.

By making the decision that we would create a consistent collection that could be sold, the communication of the entity and trademark would be carried on by the various design shops and galleries that would pick up the products.

These galleries and shops often would have their own customer bases and promotional press efforts; this would in turn effectively aid in the communication of the trademark and products even after the initial exhibition had ended. If we could attain a level of success with the collection, a constant presence could be maintained in the various galleries around the world. We also began then to realize that the trademark was in fact an infrastructure that we could build on to feed and create future projects to aid in communication efforts for the Centre.

Since we first exhibited in Maison et Objet, the collection has been exhibited extensively and is currently being represented by a number of notable galleries and design retailers worldwide.

Insights:

Although the intentions and purpose of the d.lab initiative is about the communication and showcase of the Centre's design and production capabilities, the subsequent business of production management, distribution, promotion, client and press liaising was as real as any fully fledged commercial product brand.

These activities in turn gave the team a huge amount of experience and insight into the nature of a design business; these insights could not have been realized if the very first Corian® outcomes from the Objects and Accessories Workshop stayed simply as design exercises.

Experiences from dealing with various channels (businesses, galleries, museums and the press) collected through the years are currently and frequently fed back to be incorporated into the industrial design programme at the University in the form of the various design studios.

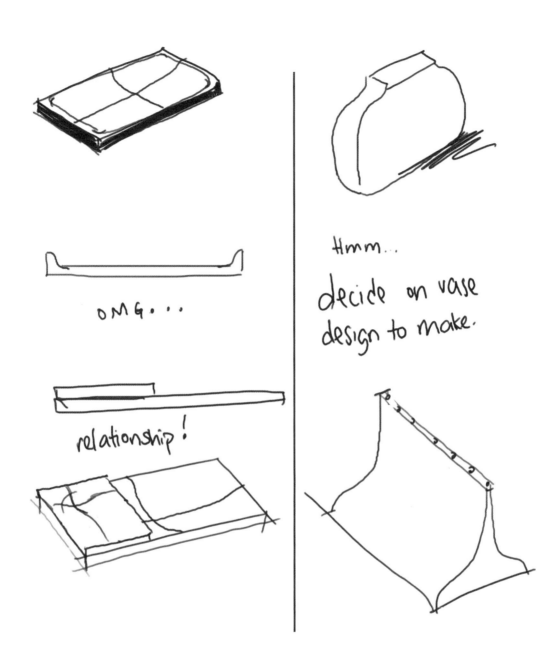

OMG...

relationship!

Hmm...

decide on vase
design to make.

Concept sketches with fabrication notes

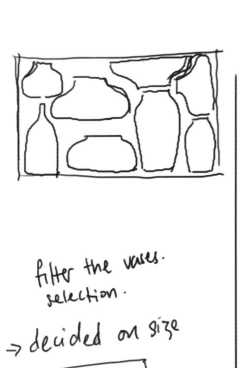

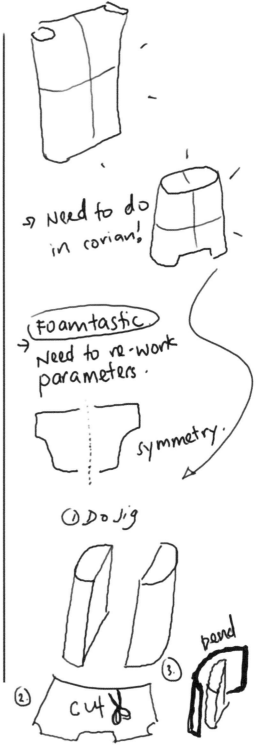

filter the vases.
selection.

→ decided on size

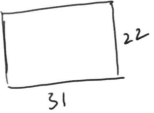

22

31

→ Sketch idea of a
vase

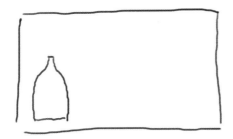

→ Need to do
in corian!

→ Foamtastic
Need to re-work
parameters.

symmetry.

① Do Jig

② cut ✂

③. bend

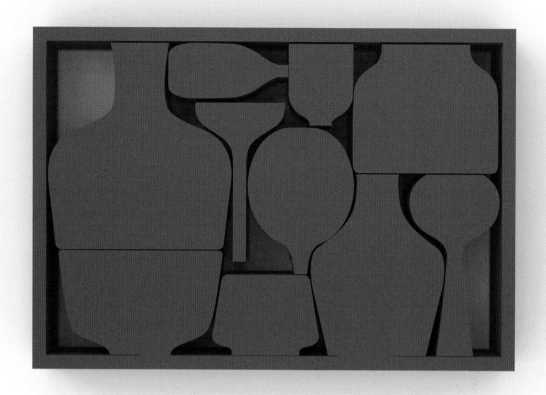

Idea of a Vase
Teak or matte-finished Corian®
W 360 x D 250 x H 45 mm

A Long Fruit Bowl
Matte-finished Corian®
W 790 x D 180 x H 90 mm
In collaboration with Dominic Poon, Tan Jun Yuan, Liang Yanjie

Round Bowl with Teak Base
Matte-finished Corian® and teak
Ø 270 x H 65 mm

Round Bowl with Teak Base, side profile view

Initiatives, Platforms and Fellowships

Layered Plates
Matte-finished Corian® and teak
W 270 x D 270 x H 85 mm

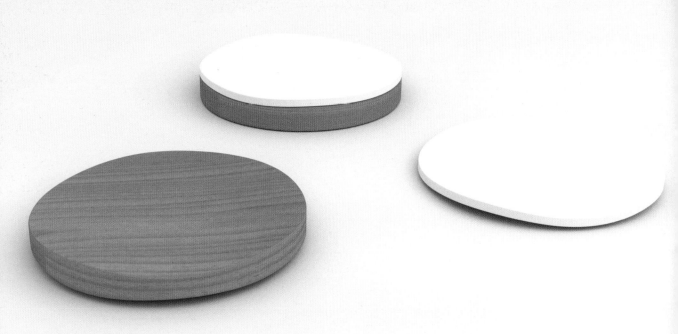

A Family of Short-Legged Lights
Matte-finished Corian®
W 470 x D 100 x H 145 mm
W 250 x D 160 x H 370 mm

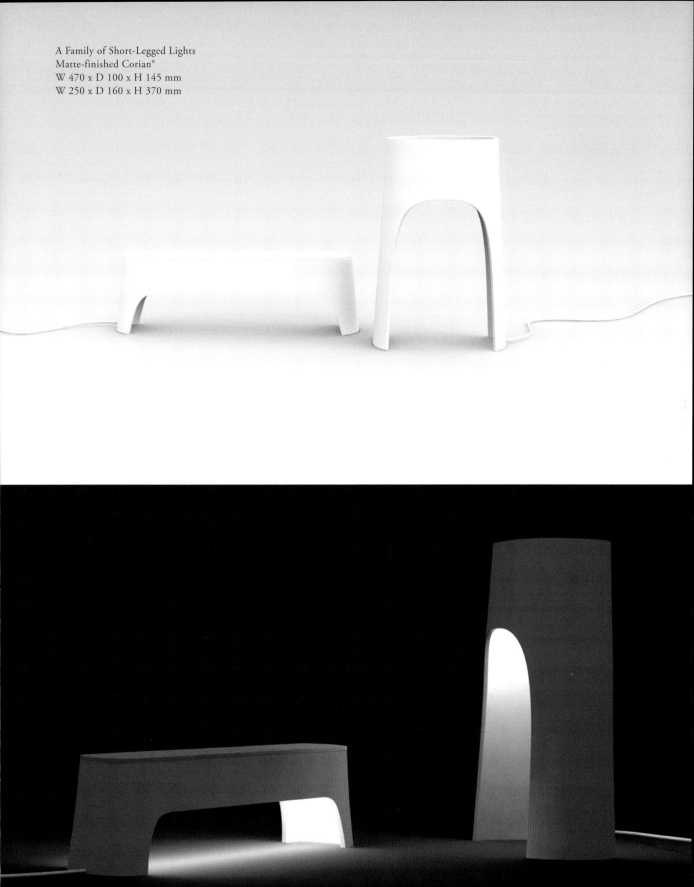

Stacking Trays
Matte-finished Corian®
W 90 x D 230 x H 17 mm
W 230 x D 230 x H 26 mm
W 320 x D 230 x H 40 mm

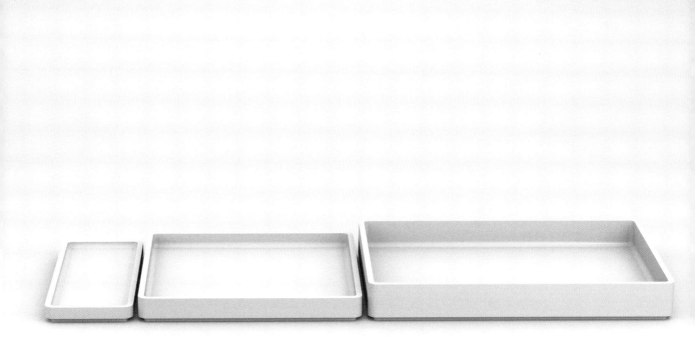

Stacking Trays, top view

Initiatives, Platforms and Fellowships

B1 and B2 lamp stock parts before assembly. Serialized
production of objects also utilizes the same processes used
to create the one-off prototypes.

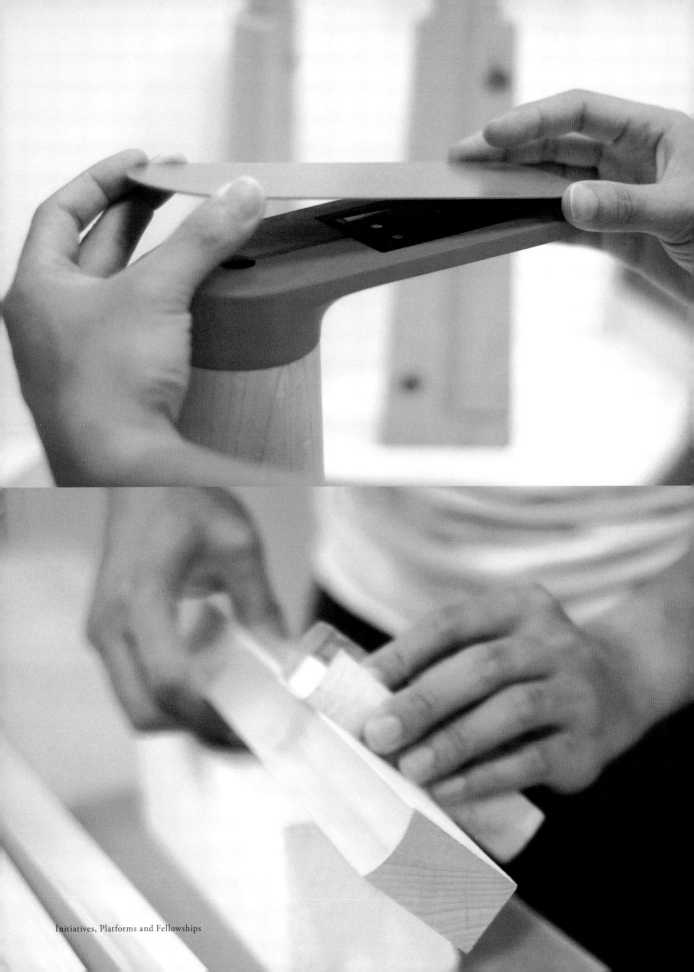

Initiatives, Platforms and Fellowships

B1 and B2 Lights
Maple, teak or aluminium, matte paint finish
W 263 x D 93 x H 250 mm
W 225 x D 98 x H 337 mm

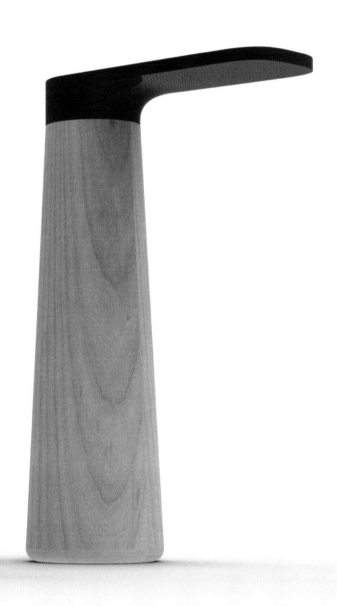

Square Block, Rectangular Block
Stationery blocks in maplewood
W 225 x D 225 x H 60 mm
W 300 x D 140 x H 60 mm

Lamp Blocks
Maple, steel, gloss paint finish
W 230 x D 77 x H 293 mm
W 165 x D 77 x H 363 mm

Pencil Block
Maple or Corian®
W 206 x D 60 x H 25 mm

Pencil Block, side profile view

Initiatives, Platforms and Fellowships

Soft Bowls
SLS nylon
W 153 x D 158 x H 80 mm
W 198 x D 205 x H 76 mm
W 249 x D 249 x H 70 mm
W 307 x D 318 x H 60 mm

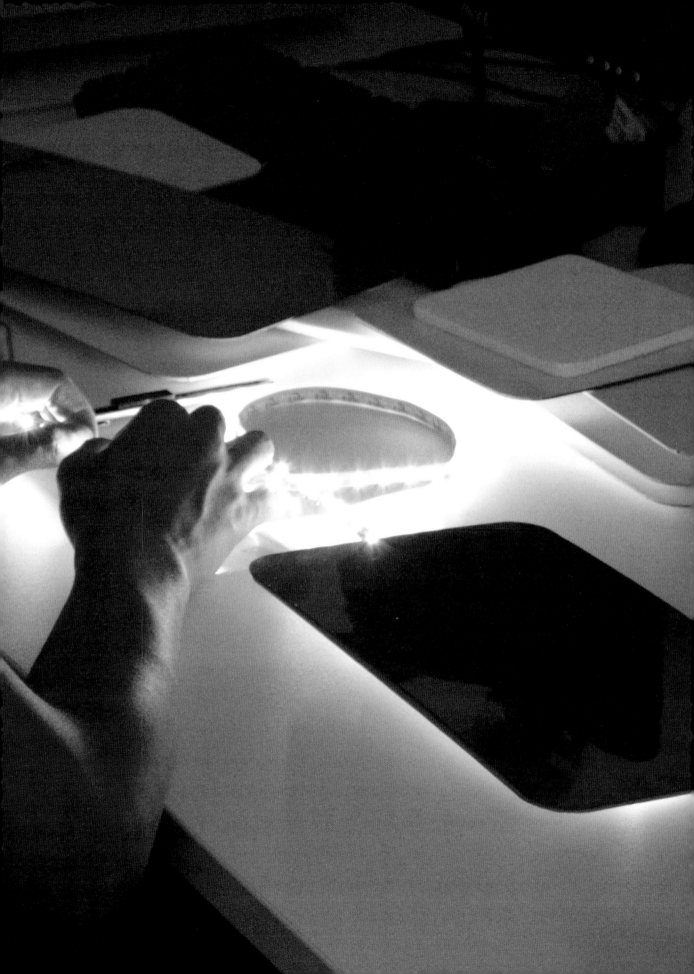

Shh Lamp
Maple
W 130 x D 70 x H 200 mm

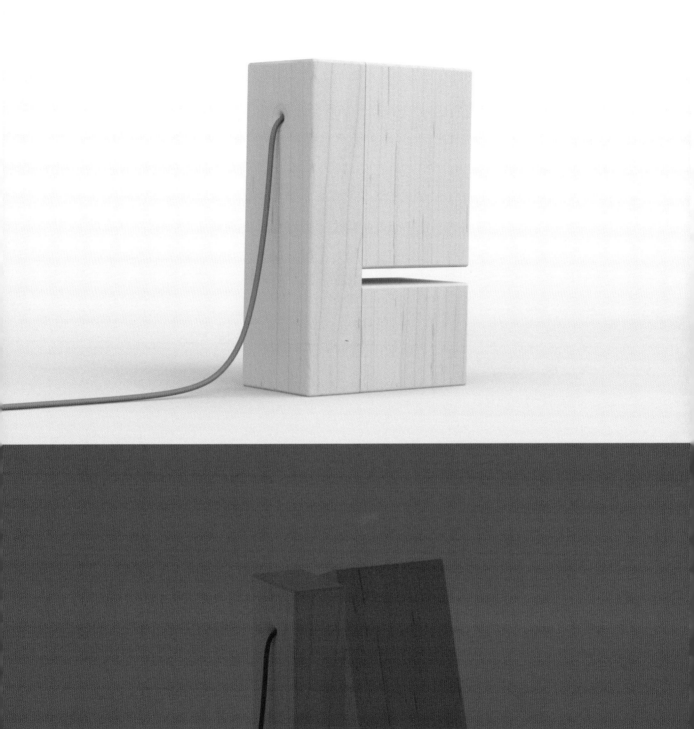

Monoplates
Corian®
W 130 x D 70 x H 200 mm

Monoplates, side profile view

Initiatives, Platforms and Fellowships

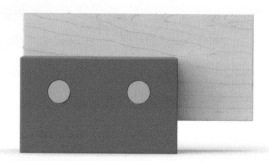

Blik and Blok
Maple, matte paint finish
W 270 x D 95 x H 157 mm

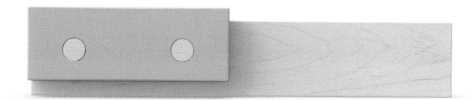

Initiatives, Platforms and Fellowships

Form and arrangement studies
built from found objects for d.lab's
pre-editions collection.

Initiatives, Platforms and Fellowships

t Light
Matte finished Corian® base, maplewood
W 240 x D 140 x H 196 mm

Initiatives, Platforms and Fellowships

4.7 Kilos of Copper,
3.65 Kilos of Copper
Copper
W 120 x D 120 x H 155 mm
W 90 x D 90 x H 220 mm

Towers
Copper
W 100 x D 100 x H 122 mm
W 222 x D 208 x H 378 mm

Copacabana
Maple and matte paint-finished aluminium
W 575 x D 210 x H 102 mm

Thick Bowl, Thicker Bowl
Matt finished Delrin®
W 150 x D 150 x H 125 mm
W 240 x D 240 x H 160 mm

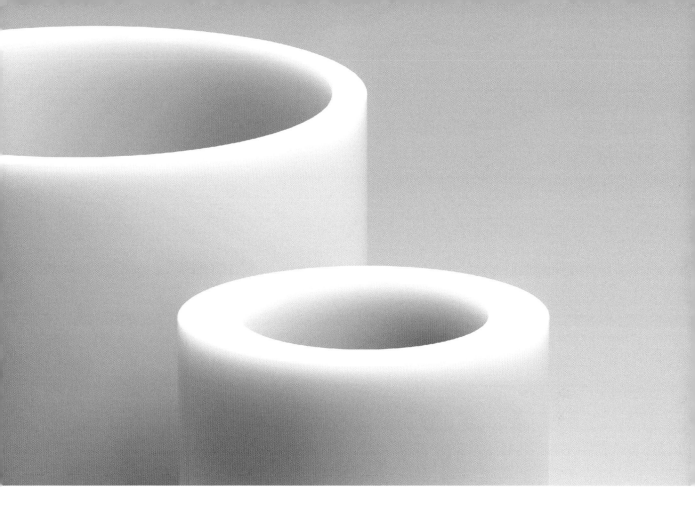

Thick Bowl, Thicker Bowl, detail

Initiatives, Platforms and Fellowships

Stick
Matte paint-finished aluminium
and matte-finished Delrin®
W 170 x D 170 x H 173 mm
W 170 x D 170 x H 303 mm
W 170 x D 170 x H 373 mm

Float
Matte paint-finished aluminium
and matte-finished Delrin®
W 230 x D 230 x H 398 mm
W 230 x D 230 x H 308 mm

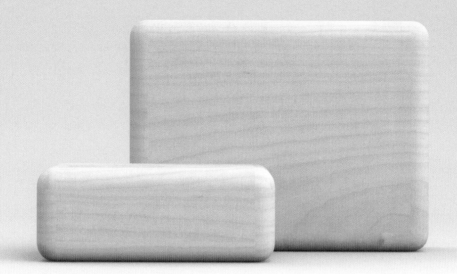

Soft Block
Maple
W 210 x D 80 x H 140 mm
W 280 x D 80 x H 210 mm

Round Block
Maple
W 230 x D 230 x H 132 mm

Glass pieces being blown by craftsmen from Tajima Glass Company, Japan

Everyday Carafe
H 270 x W 87 x D 87 mm (1.2 litres)

Everyday Glass
H 92 x W 78 x D 78 mm

Initiatives, Platforms and Fellowships

Nested Bowls
Ceramic
W 300 x D 300 x H 90 mm
W 420 x D 420 x H 40 mm
W 220 x D 220 x H 100 mm
In collaboration with ceramic artist Pearl Yang

Botanika
SLS nylon, white
Edition of 12 with 4 artist's proofs
W 110 x D 110 x H 127 mm
Originally commissioned by Bombay Sapphire

Initiatives, Platforms and Fellowships

Initiatives, Platforms and Fellowships

d.lab collections at the 2008 Maison et Objet exhibition in Paris, France

OBJECTS
AROUND
THE TABLESCAPE

d.lab

Initiatives, Platforms and Fellowships

Initiatives, Platforms and Fellowships

OBJECTS
AROUND
THE TABLESCAPE

d.lab™

Afterthoughts:

Precise, flawless, extraordinary—products that look exactly like the digital renderings; these are characteristics that have been attributed to the nature and visual language of d.lab's collections. These are not inaccurate representations of what d.lab is, but instead form only one aspect in which they are encountered and experienced.

The essence of all d.lab products originates from the idea of honesty: to the material we use, the techniques involved in shaping that material and to the designer's comprehension of form and understanding of that material's potential.

A designer's hand should be an empathetic extension that understands, distils and frames the native qualities that the material holds. Likewise, the precise fabrication by CNC machines forms part of that honesty and respect; the time and effort spent to create and produce an object from a valued material should naturally be a part of the process that distils and frames that material, without wastage or futility.

To offer the other dimension in which d.lab can be experienced, we can describe it as such: truth, purity and understanding. Objects that respect their origin and honour the qualities and personality of the materials from which they were made.

As designers, so often do we build our worlds on layers of influences and points of reference, which we take and depart from to ideate, create and design, that nothing is entirely original. A new 'language of form' was never found or discovered. What we did find instead was a position; a unique vantage point that gave us renewed insight into perceiving what an object was, is and could be.

By sharpening the focus on a product's nuances and the richness of its material composition, we created an opportunity for the viewer and consumer to readjust their paradigms of assessment and their lenses of appreciation.

Within a saturated and noisy design marketplace, this vantage point allowed us an opportunity and a means to amplify the quieter, more honest aspects of what object design really is in essence: form, material and understanding.

Beifa

How can one define and claim one's design sovereignty?

Background:

The Centre was invited by the Ningpo Industrial Design Investment and Development Company to establish an office in the new design district that was being developed. During a research trip made there, we were introduced to several local companies with which we could possibly work. Ningpo was one of the key stationery-producing cities in China and the world, and there we were introduced to Beifa, the largest stationery brand and company in Ningpo.

From our visits and conversations with Beifa, we realized that one of the biggest challenges the company faced was the creation of a consistent brand and product image in a quick-shifting industry. We then began to delve into the idea of how Beifa could lay claim to the designs they had created. The main issue at hand was the idea that brand or 'design sovereignty' was more important and had to be addressed instead of the mere design of an object.

Deconstructing the pen, we identified that the basic structural form of the pen was the most constant and recognizable form and product identity that the consumer would encounter on a frequent basis. In response to this, our strategy was to develop and design a modular pen whose basic structure and shape would remain the same but which could adapt to multiple possibilities and appeal to different trends and specific customer bases.

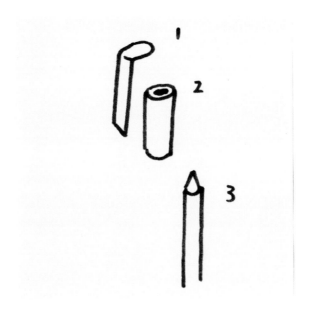

A concept sketch for the basic structure of the pen.

BEIFA

One pen connecting the world.

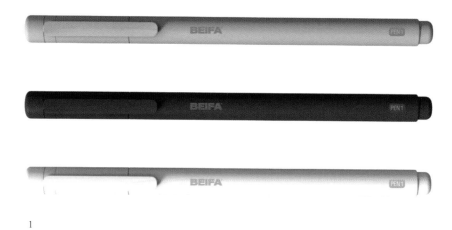

1

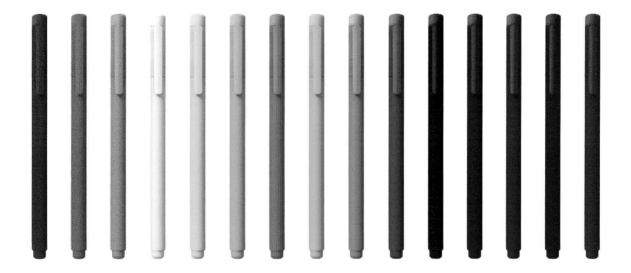

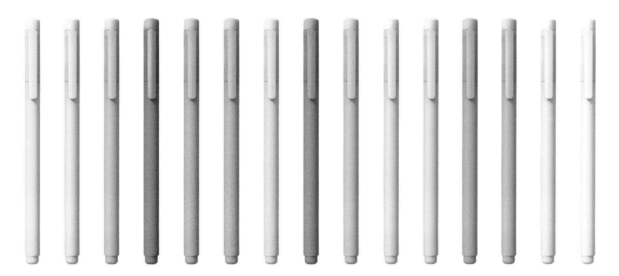

2

1 Beifa basic in black, white and grey.
2 Extension from basic colours to 48 colours.

1 2 3 4

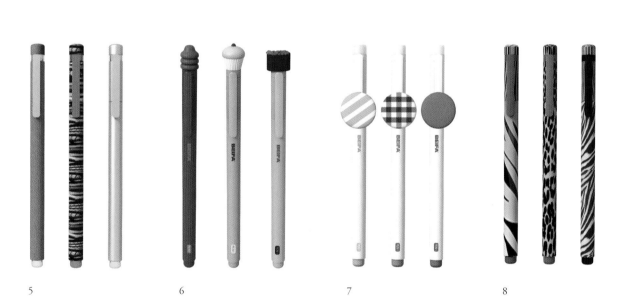

5 6 7 8

9

1 Drawing reference from familiar seasonal fashion colours: Nordic colours.
2 Proposed collaboration with a lifestyle sneaker brand.
3 Subculture inspired prints.
4 Co-branding possibilities through collaborations with scent companies.
5 Materials associated with luxury.
6 Accessorizing through trinkets.
7 Accessorizing through badges and pins.
8 In-trend fashion prints.
9 Basic prints in the permanent collection: simple black and white patterns.

Tapping into the prevalent behaviour of spinning and flicking a pen, we developed a pen with counterweights on the ends, making it much easier for a user to spin and twirl the pen around.

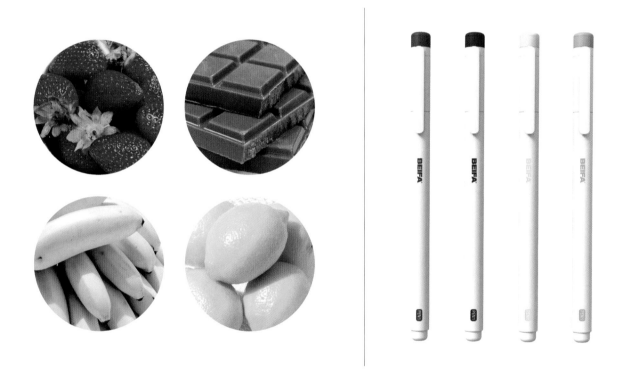

Emotive Scent
A collection of pens which carry delicious scents, awakening not only the sense of smell, but also the sense of taste. Possibilities include using scented plastic and scented inks. This will be a way of driving new technical developments within Beifa.

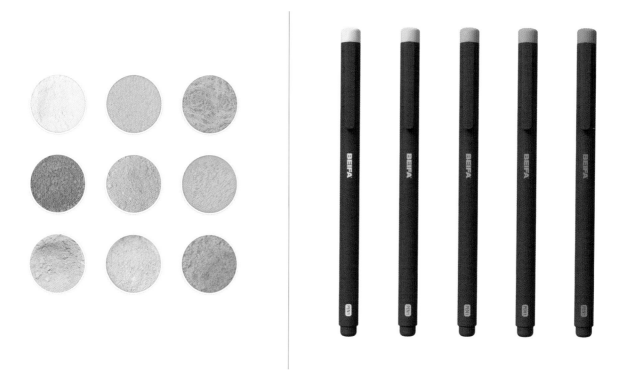

Emotive Colour

The palette of colours chosen remind the consumer of familiar shopping experiences. Inspired by sensitively chosen colours from the cosmetics and fashion industries, a consumer can be expected to find delight in choosing the right colour for herself.

Perigot

Background:

Through exhibiting consistently over the years, d.lab has managed to create and build a strong reputation; this in turn has attracted a number of parties and companies that have identified with the design philosophy and identity of d.lab and have shown interest in initiating collaborations.

A regular exhibitor at the annual Maison et Objet showcase, Perigot is a brand and company that we have come to know quite well over the years. When Perigot first approached us for a collaboration, we expressed keen interest, as we have not worked on products that are similar to theirs before, and their market appeal is significantly different from that of d.lab's. It was an interesting prospect for the team to discover if the sensibility and approach taken for d.lab could be successfully transferred to another product category.

As we began the research for Perigot, we realized that the previous design approach that was developed for the Beifa project was very relevant and had many similarities with this new commission.

The process almost always started with a thorough analysis and deconstruction of the commissioning brand to understand its history and culture. From this newfound understanding and awareness, a series of in-depth trend reports and consumer group studies are conducted to gain a deeper insight and possibly identify what might be the next big product that the market would welcome, or would have the potential to rise to become the next flagship product for the brand.

These findings eventually evolved into an opportunity for us to relook at and question the very essence of the identity that d.lab represented that attracted such collaborators to us.

Was it about the pared-back and restrained aesthetic and characteristics, the technical precision inherent in the products? Or was it about how each object would relate to its surroundings and to each other?

Concept 1: Arrangement

By reflecting on these questions we returned to one of the early points of inspiration for d.lab, a series of formal design exercises and studies outlined in the book *Elements of Design* by Rowena Reed Kostellow. By returning to this source, the essence of d.lab was confirmed: the object collections were essentially studies in how the forms related with each other (as a collection) and to the backdrop they were set up on, and their innate proportions and volumes—a study of design objects and their relationships.

Concept 2: Sympathetic Design

The idea of a sympathetic design product or, more accurately, bags
that would be sympathetic to various contemporary living scenarios
—going to the gym, overnight travelling, weekend trips—became
another angle that influenced the final forms of the series: pure
tonal colour blocks serving specific modern functional needs.

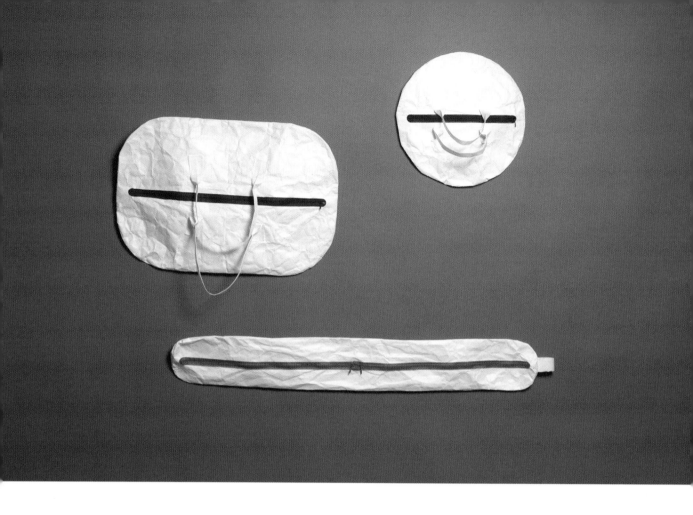

Concept 3: Product as Identity

At this point the question of the product and the brand's identity resurfaced. How could we create a distinctive, defining point of focus for the product, and ultimately the brand, without over-designing?

By re-examining the form of the bag, we noted that the pull-zipper was an integral part of the bag's overall function; by refocusing exclusively on the visual image that the zipper expresses when it becomes part of the product, we realized that it could be the representation of the product line's identity.

After resolving and identifying the definitive 'mark' for this product line, the subsequent design decisions became a series of intuitive reactions: the zipper element was further refined with subtle detailing (resulting in the rounded endings) and the application of a contrasting colour to it.

The team also chanced upon the strength and quality of Tyvek; and how the technical, flat-packing quality of the fabric allowed for a unique manner of presentation: flattened tonal blocks that could expand to large volumes.

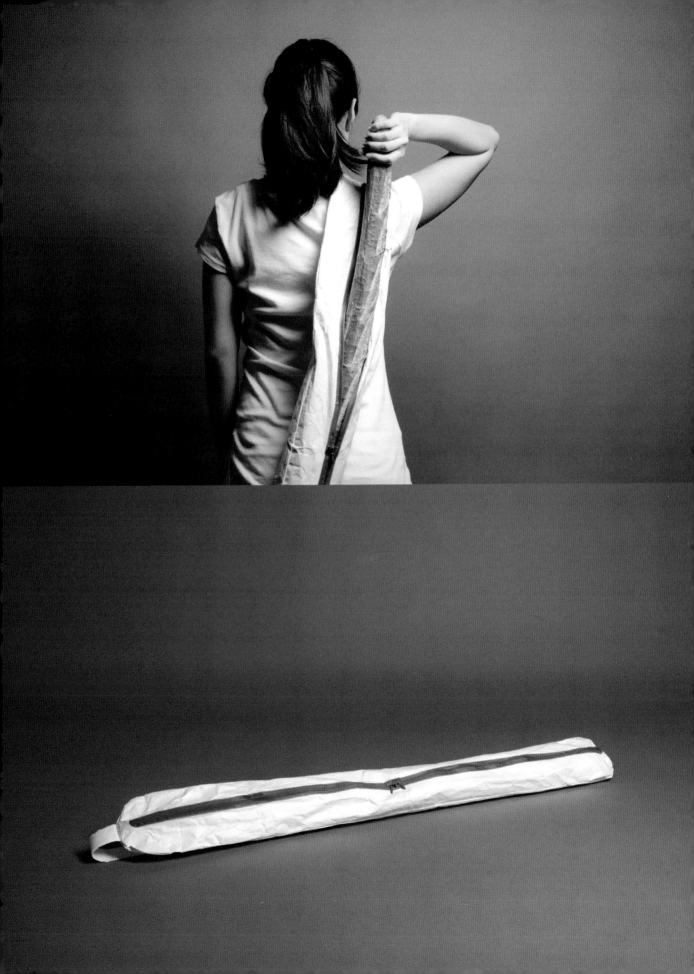

Design Fellowships

Background:

The Centre attempts to support and aid graduates and alumni of the faculty in their design activities and endeavours whenever possible. The team always searches for suitable candidates among the students through their talent, inclinations and dispositions and seeks ways in which the Centre can act as a framework to support and nurture them.

Fellowship: *Tiffany Loy*

Tiffany Loy was a graduate from the programme who was later employed as a designer with the Centre. She was instrumental in developing the Perigot project, from which she developed her own line of bags, products and fabric experiments.

We encouraged her to explore this area of interest by giving her a six-month fellowship to focus on and develop her research in fabrics and textiles by allocating a small atelier space within the current faculty's student studios. The decision to situate her atelier in the student studio space was a strategic one, an example aimed at seeding entrepreneurial behaviours in the younger students through interactions with her and her practice.

Fellowship: *Ng Aik Min*

Ng Aik Min was a graduate who was granted a research fellowship by the Centre to expand on her research thesis about incorporating plants and greenery into modern living and working spaces. Her research interests intersected with projects that the Centre was initiating at that time, and her presence as a fellow was instrumental in aiding the Centre in driving several projects and workshops.

As a direct result of her fellowship, we initiated the Workscapes Workshop, which drew together various scientists and geneticists specializing in plant research, officers from the National Environment Agency and several representatives from companies producing office furniture systems. The results, insights and interactions from the workshop eventually resulted in the Office Planner, a prototype for a new office furniture system and organizer, and a prototype moss planter, Maomao.

Opposite: Cross-section of a quilt to explore translucency in quilted fabrics; from Tiffany Loy's 'Quilted Objects' studies.

Quilted Objects

Background:

Developed as an off-tangent materials exploration venture in parallel to the work for Perigot, Quilted Objects was an investigation into the possibility of covering every hard surface with soft and quilted forms to explore and discover the potential of what a simple household production tool such as a sewing machine could do. The process of quilting, sewing and stitching opened a new direction of possibilities and the explorations were developed into a stand-alone research venture to discover new ideas for future product collections.

Various experimentations with quilting objects that surround us.

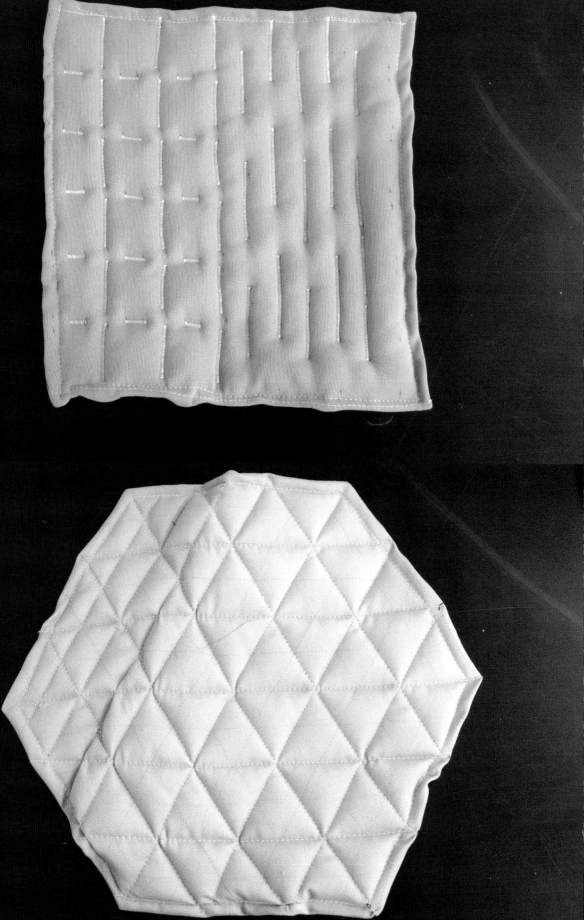

Pleats and Dye

Background:

In a workshop conducted with the faculty's students, Tiffany tapped into the students' capabilities to aid her in her research on fabrics and textiles. The workshop also became an avenue for her to transfer and teach the various tips, skills and technical know-how that she has developed to the student population.

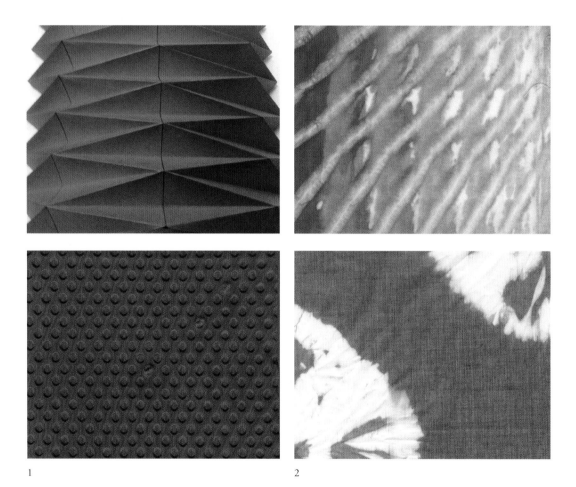

1

2

1   Various pleat patterns created from experimentation.
2   Textile dye experiments from student workshop participants.

Opposite: Detail of an embossed textile pattern.
Above: Textile crinkle experimentation producing the form of a pitta bread.

Workscapes Workshop

Background:

    The Workscapes Workshop arose from the idea of introducing greenery and plant life to transform working conditions into living conditions through rethinking the manner and paradigm in which workspaces are treated and perceived.

    The Centre's team encouraged the workshop participants' conceptualization process along the path of developing ideas that would exist as integrated parts of existing office systems and workspaces instead of being potentially disruptive additions.

Above: Research fellow Ng Aik Min working on moss experiments.
Opposite: Professor Chia Tet Fatt, an expert in plant genetics, showing his plant experiments.

Office Planner

Conceptual office spatial reconfiguration

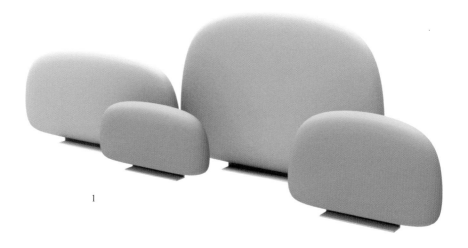

1

Background:

An office system furniture proposal for Office Planner, a Singapore-based company, this concept was developed from the moss experiments that were developed by Aik Min. The Centre's team took her basic developments and further expanded them as a divider system. Although these dividers are not actual plant life, the rounded forms and structures create a friendlier and softer mood in a workspace environment when introduced.

2

1 Bush divider system (foam and textile) for desktop systems
2 Complete overview of Office Planner office system
3 Divider system in use on single desks

3

Maomao

Self-regulating moss planter

1

Background:

A 3D-printed prototype, Maomao was designed to be a one-off object that explored the porous qualities of sintered polyamide nylon powder prototypes in the form of a decorative planter.

Maomao originated from an observation that was drawn when the team was creating a prototype of a cup: during the design process it was noted that the cup prototype seemed to be drawing the water that was poured into it slowly outwards through capillary action, resulting in the outer surface of the cup actually becoming damp and moist.

2

1   Moss plants both physically and biologically
    supported by the nylon base below.
2   Internal nylon structures which elevate the moss
    plants from the water reservoir beneath.

Studio Juju

An independent design spin-off

Studio Juju is a design partnership formed by Timo Wong and Priscilla Lui in 2009 when both were working as designers in the Centre. Through their work for the various d.lab collections, the Centre encouraged the duo to independently develop, create and exhibit their own collection in Milan's SaloneSatellite. In 2010, Studio Juju became independent and have since continued to develop projects for clients both locally and internationally.

Bambi Chair
Rabbit and Tortoise

Duck Lamp

5 TRANSPORATION DESIGN AND PROTOTYPING CAPABILITIES

As we move forward, many of our projects are shifting away from form-based design styling into the area of service and experience design, in which the designed object frequently exists only as a small part of the total solution, and sometimes not at all. However, we still find ourselves drawn to the idea of making a beautiful sketch or sculpting a beautiful and emotive object with our hands.

The concept car is probably the epitome of this form of design pursuit, an evocative object that represents the synthesis of engineering, artistry and craftsmanship.

Through our collaborations with the Department of Mechanical Engineering at the National University of Singapore, the Centre had the opportunity to indulge in the ultimate fantasies of many young design students. This concept car collaboration has also provided us with a platform to develop other projects built around the framework of mobility in urban environments and to look at transportation as a total system beyond the design of a single vehicle.

The skills and abilities required to design and build a concept car represent the highest level of traditional industrial design with regard to the areas of form-giving, control of lines and surface highlighting. As designers, we believe these abilities and skills are what define and set us apart from being just design thinkers, and we strive to develop them at the highest level.

Through these projects, we have also built up a suite of different prototyping capabilities that allow us to fluidly translate the ideas which we hold in our heads to the computer, and finally into full-sized prototypes, ready for testing and evaluation.

Design For Future Mobility

Background:

The goal of Design For Future Mobility was not to propose overly dynamic and futuristic transportation solutions but instead to present ways in which we could reframe the current paradigm and perceptions that we have of transportation; if we can begin by changing our commuting habits, it might perhaps be a step towards solving many of the problems that we face in cities presently.

Through the examination of the relationships that exist between people, vehicles and infrastructure, we identified gaps that could be closed and opportunities that we could embrace. New technologies and sensibilities will continue to affect the outlook we have on the future of mobility; by holding on to this prospect we developed designs and proposals for sustainable transportation solutions that would shape future personal travel in our cities.

Concepts:

Cycle One

A compact one-person mobility device, Cycle One provides its user with the agility needed to weave through crowds and tight urban spaces. On arrival at the destination, the user can choose either to park and lock the device or have it follow behind with the 'tag along' program function.

Cab One

Designed for the ferrying of a single passenger and for short commuting trips, Cab One is a concept born from a reconsideration of solitary commuting behaviours and patterns in dense urban cities such as Singapore. The compact and efficient nature of the vehicle's design allows it to travel at its optimum level while occupying minimal road space.

Explorer Concept Vehicle

The Explorer Concept Vehicle attempts to alter the way we travel through spaces and distances by creating a new wealth of possibilities in the travel experience. An environment as much as a vehicle, it is designed for urban dwellers looking to escape the city in search of new patterns and behaviours while travelling. Its intent is very much about the journey itself, rather than the destination.

Large panoramic windows broaden the visual range of passengers and transform dull and ordinary routes into leisurely journeys with a new pool of visual opportunities. An intelligent vehicular system offers freedom by aiding in the mapping and planning of trips without the stress.

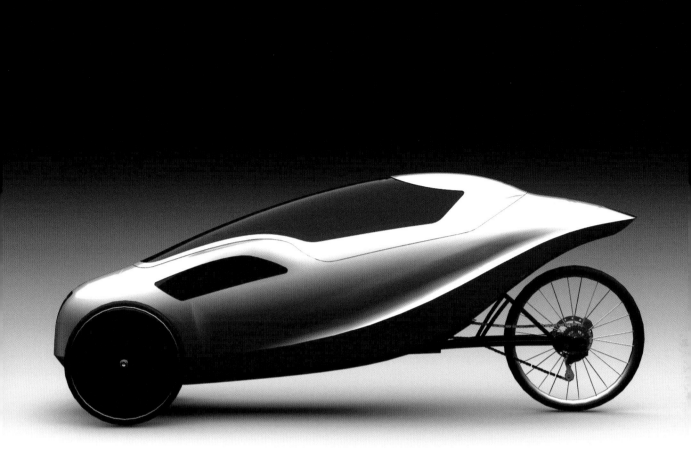

Velomobile

A Velomobile is an electric, human-powered enclosed vehicle designed to offer aerodynamic advantage and full protection from the weather and traffic collisions. The concept was derived from the idea of a recumbent tricycle, a vehicle that offers greater comfort over distances compared to a conventional two-wheel bicycle. The increasing interest in sustainable forms of travel and mobility makes the Velomobile an attractive, appealing alternative to purchasing a car or motorbike.

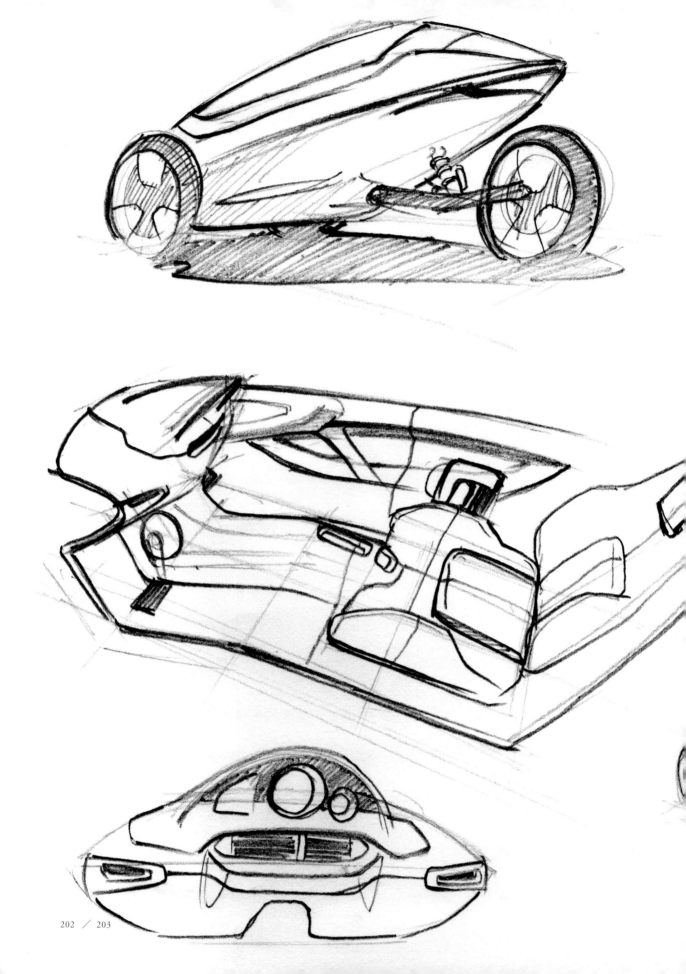

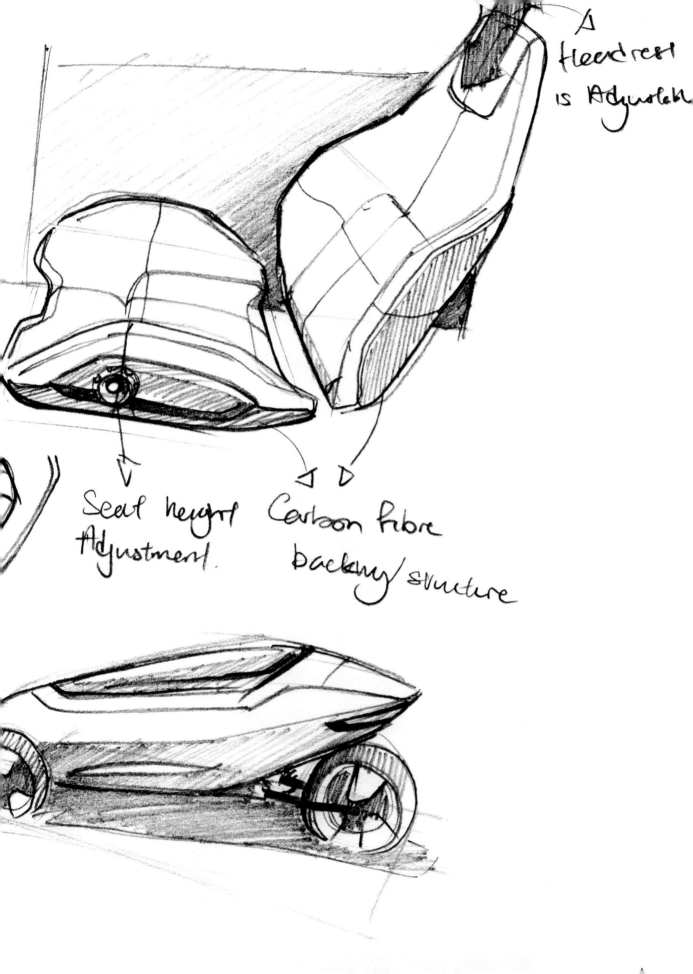

Headrest is Adjustable

Seat height Adjustment.

Carbon Fibre backing structure

NUS Urban Concept Eco Car

Background:

The NUS Urban Concept Eco Car was jointly developed by the Centre and the National University of Singapore's Department of Mechanical Engineering, for participation in the Shell Eco-marathon Europe 2008, held at the Nogaro Motor Circuit in France.

This single-seat concept car was designed to address issues of fuel efficiency and environmental impact and is designed to run on Gas-to-Liquid fuel, an alternative energy source. As a single rear-wheel drive car, the vehicle is developed with a low rolling resistance, thus enabling it to freewheel without consuming any fuel on reaching certain speed marks.

Above: NUS Urban Concept Eco Car at the racing circuit.
Opposite, top: The Eco Car in the Shell Eco-marathon race.
Opposite, bottom: Race preparations on the circuit.

NUS Kruce Eco Car

Background:

 The Kruce is the second eco concept car that was jointly developed and designed by the Centre and the NUS Department of Mechanical Engineering for the annual Shell Eco-marathon held in Europe.

 Working from insights and processes learnt while building the previous Urban Concept Eco Car, the Centre's team focused on the development of a performance-driven form and the improvement of accessibility.

 The design for Kruce is based on the metaphor of a cell—a fluid, continuous body with minimal protrusions. The overall design of the car was continuously analyzed, studied and reiterated to obtain the final, aerodynamic form.

Above: NUS Kruce Eco Car at the racing circuit.
Opposite: Initial sketches and renderings for the design.

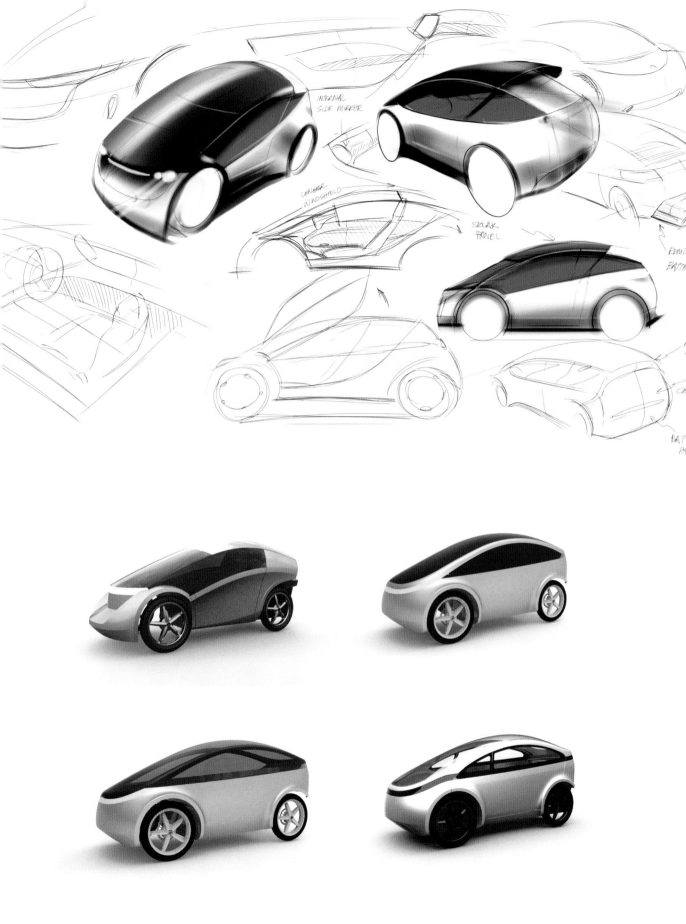

Digital Fabrication

Background:

A new manufacturing paradigm has been created: the popularity and availability of processes such as computer numerical controlled (CNC) machining and 3D printing processes, which were once used primarily for production tooling, are now increasingly being used for mass production of components and entire products themselves.

This in turn makes the prototype, which is created by such techniques, almost indistinguishable from the actual production models. This widespread availability and access frees us from the constraint of needing to adhere to economies of scale in production by enabling small research outfits such as ours to produce and create on demand.

5-Axis CNC Machining Capabilities

In Singapore, there is always a struggle and a lot of difficulty involved in getting products or objects created to exacting specifications, and this is primarily due to a distinct lack of skilled model-making craftsmen based locally.

With the acquisition of the 5-Axis CNC machines, co-funded by the Department of Mechanical Engineering, the team was able to effectively and quickly sidestep this problem: the precision of the 5-Axis machines enabled the team's designers to translate almost any designs drawn in CAD programmes precisely into physical mock-ups for immediate evaluation.

The removal of the negotiation process with external contractors and fabricators frees and enables us to create an extremely smooth and fluid process for creating design iterations; any subtle changes made in the CAD program could then be immediately translated tangibly.

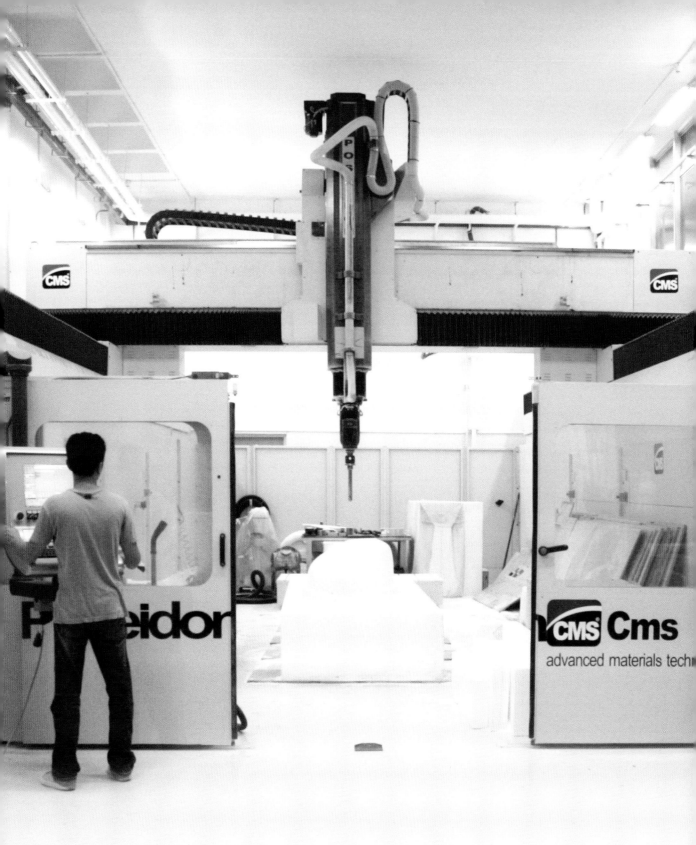

Poseidon 5-Axis CNC machine with a stroke size of 7500 x 3500 x 2000 mm

Transportation Design and Prototyping Capabilities

Transportation Design and Prototyping Capabilities

Transportation Design and Prototyping Capabilities

ABE the Tummy Dummy

Abdominal simulation device for medical students

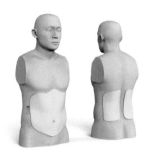

Background:

ABE the Tummy Dummy is an abdominal simulator designed to enable medical trainees to effectively practise physical examination techniques. This is especially useful when access to human patients is limited, or if patients refuse to be examined.

Primarily a collaboration project with Associate Professor Erle Lim of the Yong Loo Lin School of Medicine at the National University of Singapore, ABE aimed to produce a synthetic torso simulator that could be used for various teaching and demonstrative purposes. The process of creating Tummy Dummy gave us two key insights:

1   Production challenges faced by the Centre's team in attaining a high level of tactile realism for the creation of the Tummy Dummy led to the use of new materials and new ways of making and doing.

2   From the build-on-demand requests for Tummy Dummy products sprang a commercialization idea that would cater specifically to orders from medical training faculties and schools.

The value for the Centre's team was in the creation of new processes to integrate the various tools we had into a unified flow: the 3D scanning and digitization of an actual human torso, the subsequent manipulation and rendering of the scanned data to the final fabrication and production process using new materials to simulate the visual and tactile texture of human organs.

The approach we adopted towards creating Tummy Dummy was very much akin to the manner in which a prop- and model-building studio operates; in fact, the materials used to produce the dummy organs were actual gels that Hollywood set designers would use to create artificial organs and monsters. We were also forced to explore new sets of digital tools that were more often used by animators than industrial designers.

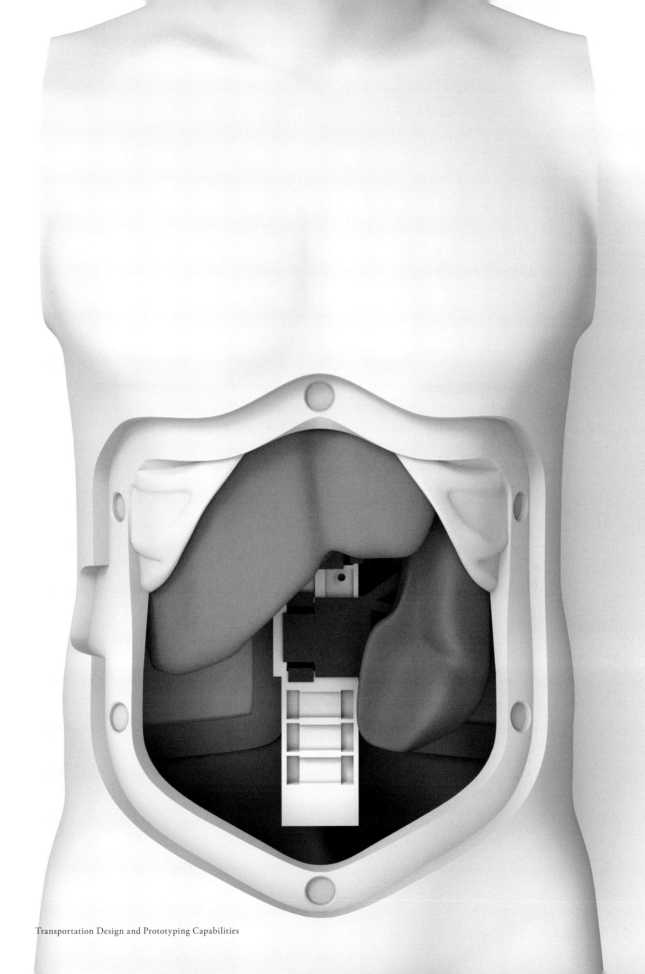

Transportation Design and Prototyping Capabilities

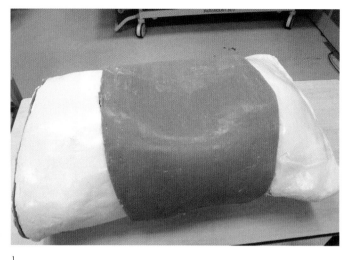

1

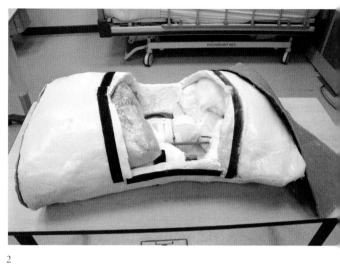

2

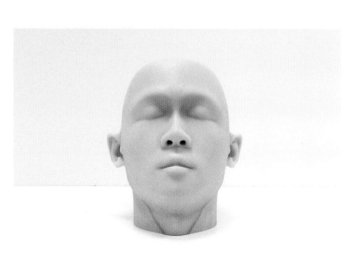

3

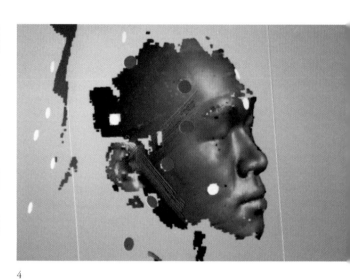

4

5

6

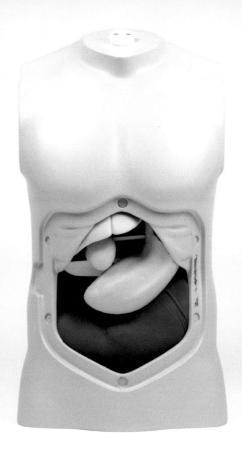

An Early Version of the Tummy Dummy

This initial iteration was a simple prototype that the tutors and students made with everyday objects and with basic production processes with which they were familiar.

Although this iteration was extremely raw in its presentation and form, it did serve the purpose of acting as a training tool. This quick and raw method of prototyping was a tool with which the Centre's team identified as similar methods are also used to quickly create proof-of-concepts.

1–2   Original Dummy made by the medical students.
3–4   3D scanning process of a live model.
5   Rapid prototyped model of a human head from scanned data.
6   Finished prototype of the first iteration made by the Centre.

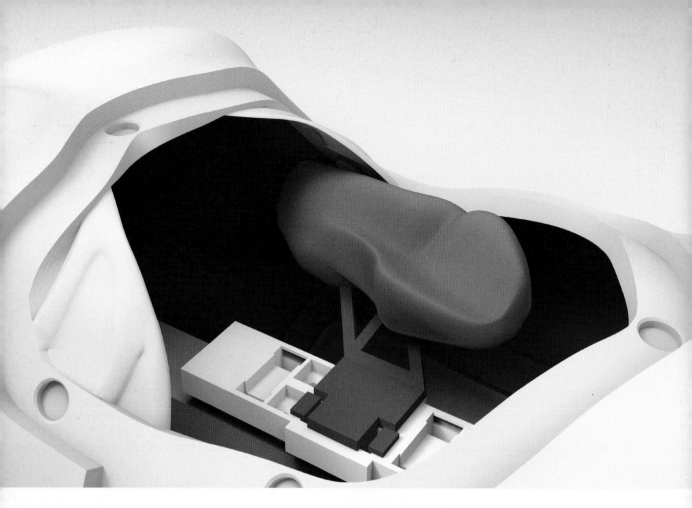

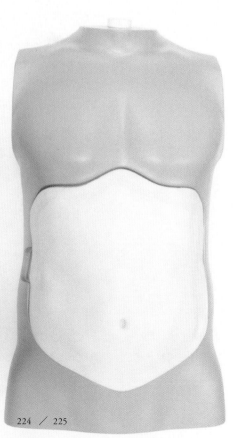

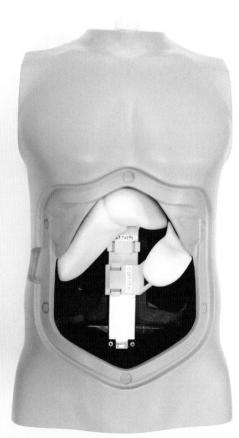

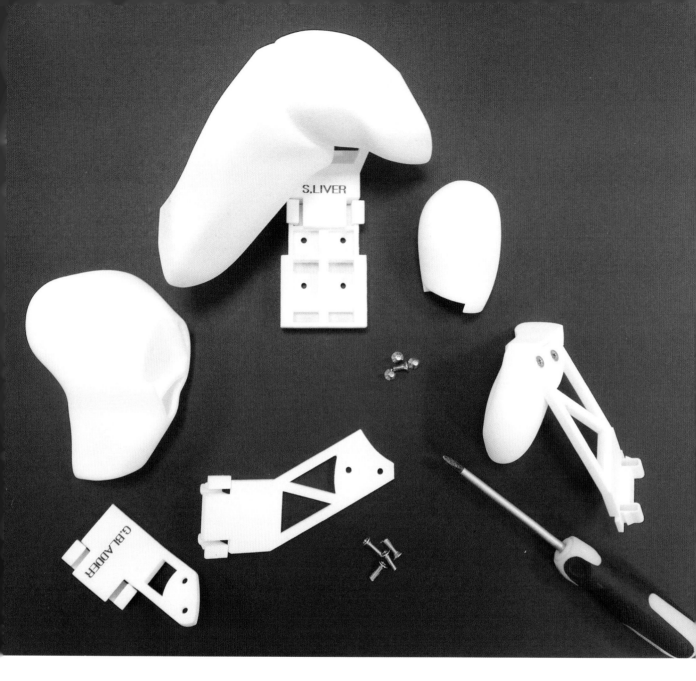

3D Printing as Production

For the latest iteration of ABE the Tummy Dummy, we produced most of the dummy organs with Shapeways, an online 3D print-on-demand service based in the Netherlands. This arrangement allows us to keep almost no inventory and stock, thus freeing us from the constraint of needing to store excess raw materials required for production.

The process also allows us to upgrade and refine the models quickly as each new version produced will be informed by the latest feedback or information from customers. Through this collaborative dynamic of feedback and insight, our customers also become our collaborators.

6 A FEEDBACK LOOP FOR PRACTICE AND TEACHING

The Design Platforms were introduced to include a more responsive and adaptive teaching structure into the Industrial Design Programme at the National University of Singapore.

This structure enables the faculty to respond quickly to the demands of new emergence within design by introducing new projects or topics each semester. This structure also enables the faculty to bring in experts and collaborators fairly quickly when the opportunities present themselves.

Besides transferring the knowledge, skills set and experience acquired from our research and practice to the teaching programme, the Centre also taps into its own resources to help develop new areas of the teaching programme which are beyond the practice and expertise of our current faculty.

Transportation Studio   *with Ulrich Schraudolph*

Studio Synopsis:

An exercise in finding new ways of creating meaningful and effective inter-faculty collaborations, this studio covered the topic of electric transportation. With an electric vehicle platform as the only project constraint, students from Mechanical Engineering and Industrial Design worked in small teams to develop concept cars that would take references and inspiration from the following: emerging technology, new social behaviours and existing infrastructure.

Zeleritas
Willie Tay, Chew Lee Fon, Pan Yu and Wong Mun Teng

An electric car platform developed for local racing subcultures, creating a driving experience that is thrilling and highly sensorial.

A Feedback Loop for Practice and Teaching

Interactive Play Studio

with Ulrich Schraudolph and Yuta Nakayama

Studio Synopsis:

Usability in interaction design is a buzzword that has been floating around for a while, but in truth the realization of a truly immersive interactive digital experience is probably still in its infant stages. In order for true progressive developments to take place, the interactive concepts developed need to go through an exploratory phase that concerns itself with 'what can be done, and how' before focusing on resolving the technicalities of the design. In this Studio students explored the idea of multi-sensorial interactivity through the design of conceptual games, exhibits and installations that were not limited by 'realistic' constraints.

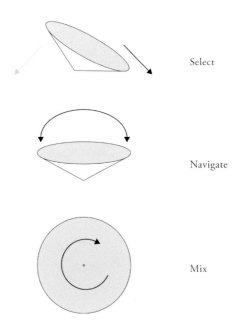

Select

Navigate

Mix

Hacking Orchestra
Pierre-Loup Dumas and Zoe Aegerter (exchange students from ENSCI-Les Ateliers,
École Nationale Supérieure de Création Industrielle, Paris, France)

A concept composed of two interactive objects, the Wand and the Conductor, which 'play' with other objects and the sounds they produce. The Wand and the Conductor interact together to produce a succession of transformed sounds, which become melodies.

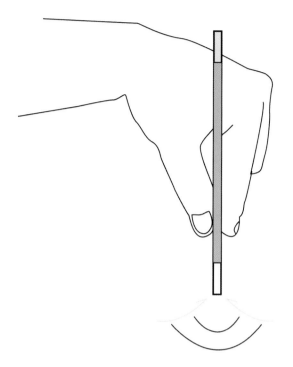

Recording Sounds

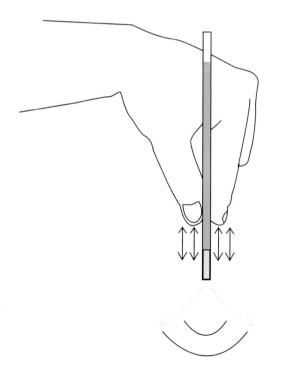

Restituting Sound
Automatic Looping Sound

Speaker
Microphone
Accelerometer
Gyrometer

Trends Studio *with Lim Marn*

Studio Synopsis:

> The Trends Studio saw us working with Lim Marn, a materials and colour specialist, who we invited to collaborate with us on this project. Students were asked to analyze current and past trends in design, fashion, arts, architecture, science, technology, literature, philosophy and social phenomena, and to identify an emerging trend that could be translated into a new programme for a product line. Insights that were obtained from d.lab exhibition experiences overseas were used to inform the students.

Peculiar Attachments
Chung Sui Fai

The usage of unconventional joining elements in design objects was identified as an emerging trend. Peculiar Attachments sought to capitalize on this by making the unconventional joints a key design feature.

A design philosophy that goes against the grain of current design trends

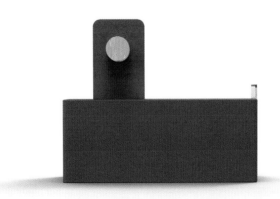

Sheet Metal Studio *with Werner Aisslinger and Lim Marn*

Studio Synopsis:

Student participants were asked to develop a project outcome that works within the constraints and possibilities offered by the process of laser cutting and folding sheet metal aluminium. Though utilizing a fairly low-cost and cheap production process, the resulting objects had to contain a certain aesthetic value and functional worth relevant to today's domestic context and environment.

Purée de carottes
Marie Douel (exchange student from ECAL, Lausanne, Switzerland)

Inspired by the mesh structure, the basket takes advantage of its elasticity and the metal's resistance, creating a movable object in which the elements are highly structured but still sensual and fluid when pieced together.

Generative Design Studio

Studio Synopsis and Background:

We have an ongoing fascination with forms that are created by algorithms; mind-boggling shapes that cannot be imagined by the mind but paradoxically contain a sense of order and logic to the way they are structured. The Generative Design Studio is an exploration in developing these forms with the aid of algorithmic software and digital fabrication techniques.

At the Centre, there were several initial attempts to create and design objects with complex forms through the use of open-source parametric software; however, the results were less than pleasing and we did not get very far. Projecting on how we could create a more focused effort, we decided to tap into the talents of the students by creating the Generative Design Studio, which would introduce and explore this subject in greater depth.

At that time, many students were also beginning to explore the aesthetic possibilities of generative forms but were having difficulty in the building and construction of the forms physically; the Generative Design Studio thus became a focal point for both the students and the Centre to pool their resources to have a more concentrated attempt at this subject matter.

Sine Shade
Clement Zheng

The sine shade was an exploration into the dynamic formal qualities of the sine wave. Concentric chains of sine-wave oscillations, coupled with flexible sintered nylon material, create a mesh that expands and contracts. The rigidity of the mesh varies radially, giving the form a certain structural quality.

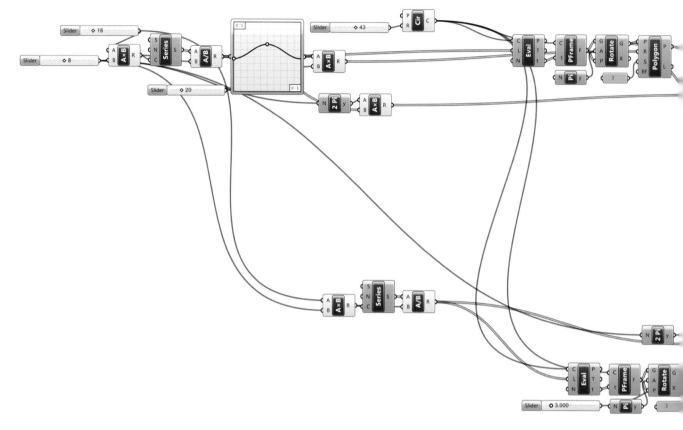

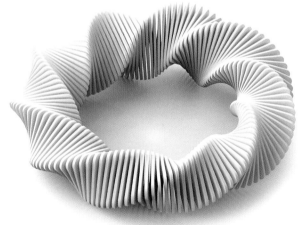

Triangles
Clement Zheng

This triangular section spring exploits the flexibility
of the nylon sintering rapid prototyping, generating a
visually rigid but highly flexible form.

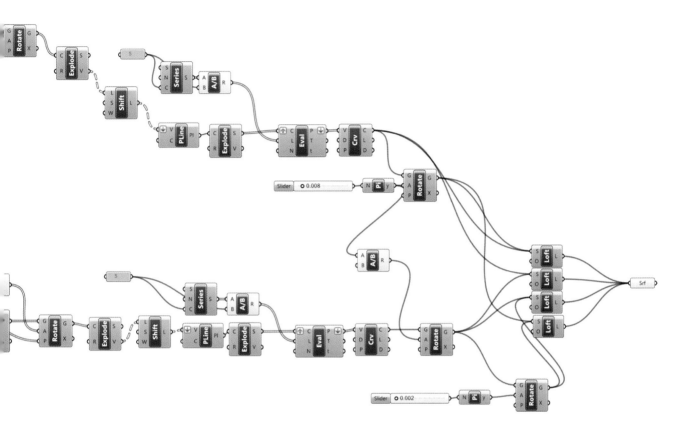

Above: A visual algorithm written in the Grasshopper
software for the Triangles prototype.

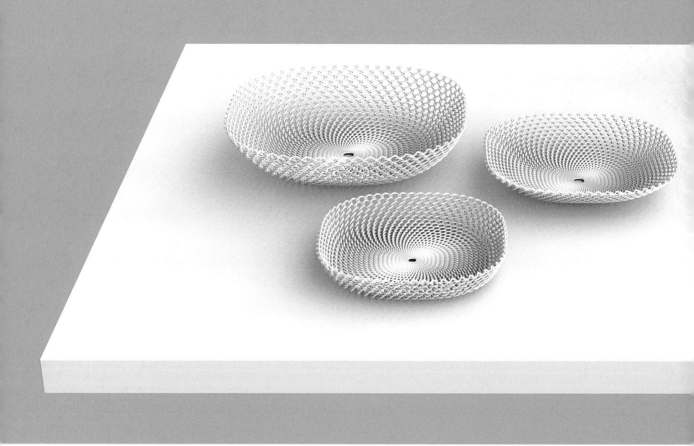

Sine Dishes
Clement Zheng

A family of vessels generated from the humble sine-wave oscillation. The
mathematical control over the weaving pattern blurs the line between the hand-
crafted and digitally fabricated, resulting in a series of objects with a visual
lightness beyond conventional weaving techniques.

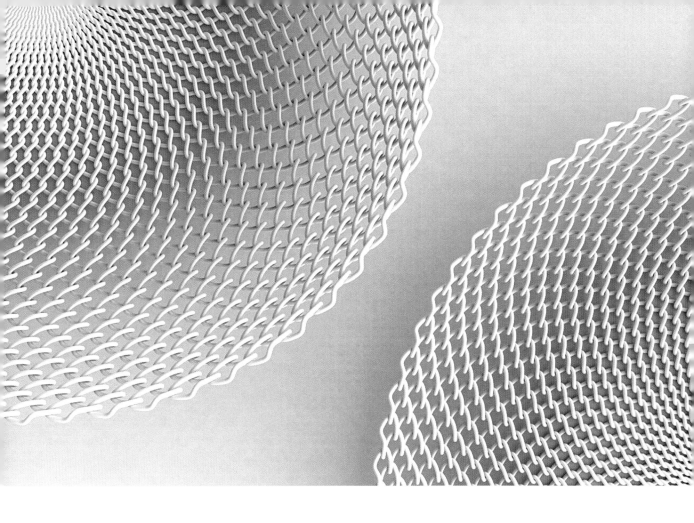

A Feedback Loop for Practice and Teaching

d.lab 2.0 *with Yong Jieyu*

Studio Synopsis:

Essentially a design platform that sought to define and explore new directions and possibilities for d.lab, students were given the opportunity to create objects and collections that might possibly bring the d.lab brand into the next stage. The Centre sought to create a new sense of ownership within the existing student body towards d.lab by engaging and bringing them in to partake in the future of the brand.

Above: Baker's Block *by Min Hwe*
Opposite, top: Dome Collection *by Wang Ying Hsuan*
Opposite, below: Silver Droplets *by Nur Azizah binte Abdullah*

Within an Arrangement, development prototypes *by Cai Zhixiang*

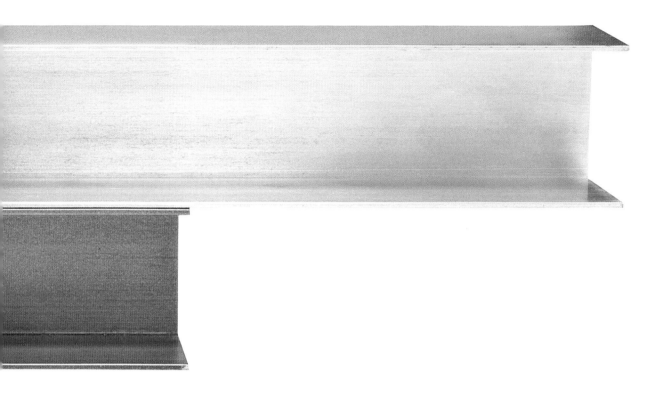

Afterthoughts:

With the advent of open-source digital platforms, online forums, communities, services such as YouTube and talks delivered at broadcasted events like TED, anyone could learn almost everything on the Internet.

How do we then tap into these tools to support our teaching? Or perhaps more accurately, how do we, as design educators and institutions, re-tool ourselves to fit into these new ecosystems of learning?

EPILOGUE

What will the future design practice be,
and how do we shape and prepare for it?

The role of design is evolving very quickly as designers are constantly finding themselves engaging in new domains which demand a different set of tools, skill sets and, more importantly, fresh mindsets.

As design practitioners we need to develop tools to manage and adapt to this flux. As design educators we need to prepare the future designer for these challenges.

The challenge of the future will be about design implementation. Design does not exist by itself, and many of these new projects will require new frameworks and new mindsets for them to be implemented successfully. The ability of a designer to engage various stakeholders will be more critical than ever.

The future practice of design seems to demand a designer who is both intuitive and analytical: the designer has to be able to move between the micro and macro, to be nimble and fluid, and be comfortable with outlining the big strategy in one instance and, in the next, be also able to make the right decision on the smallest detail, such as making the call on a 2.5mm radius versus a 2.0mm radius, a detail which can make or break a product.

With new challenges come new opportunities. The advent of new technology and new business platforms have offered many new opportunities that were not available before for today's creators. For example, web-based platforms such as Kickstarter have offered new ways for a content creator to get their project funded and realized. 3D printing on demand with online service bureaux has allowed us to produce parts without investing heavily in tooling costs. Many designers are now moving away from the fee-for-service model to that of a design knowledge-for-equity stake model, or designer-as-entrepreneur model, co-investing and setting up businesses producing their own creations.

We also see a future where design education becomes a form of basic education. The young, equipped with new skills and ways of thinking offered by design training, will then start new specializations in engineering, science, biology, medicine, economics, business, and so forth, thus creating a new hybrid of design-trained specialists who will bring a paradigm shift to their respective domains.

Big Data. Teaming. Hacking, Tinkering and Coding. Design Thinking 2.0. Tools to Nudge Habit and Behaviour. These are some of the new areas of investigation which the Centre is currently embarking on.

As we once again launch ourselves into the unknown, we hope that we will continue to find new and exciting possibilities for the practice of design.

ACKNOWLEDGEMENTS

The Centre would not have existed without the vision and funding of the management of the National University of Singapore (NUS).

All projects and workshops would not have been possible without the support and contribution from our colleagues, collaborators, workshop participants, retailers, supporting government agencies, collectors, press, vendors, contractors and students.

Special thanks to Professor Tan Chorh Chuan, President of NUS and Professor Tan Eng Chye, Deputy President (Academic Affairs) and Provost, for their generous and continous support for the Centre.

Special thanks to Professor Heng Chye Kiang, Dean of the School of Design and Environment, who masterminded the establishment of the Centre and for giving me this fantastic opportunity.

To Professor Cheong Hin Fatt, immediate former-Dean of the School of Design and Environment, who told me to be brave and to 'just do it'.

To my colleagues and partners-in-crime Associate Professor Yen Chin Chiuan and Associate Professor Christian Boucharenc.

I would also like to extend my gratitude to all fellow colleagues from the Division of Industrial Design Programme, especially to Donn Koh, Clement Zheng, Winnie Chin and Avril Teh.

To Associate Professor Wong Yunn Chii, for the trust and guidance during the Centre's years in the Department of Architecture. To the support staff of the Department of Architecture: Ms Goh Lay Fong, Ms Rozita bte Ahmad, Mrs Margaret Wong, Ms Dorothy Man, Mr Sek Siak Chiang, Ms Cindy Tan, Mr Mohd Sah bin Sadon, Mr Muji bin Hochri.

To colleagues from the Department of Mechanical Engineering: Professor Lim Seh Chun, Professor Wong Yoke San, Professor Jerry Fuh, Associate Professor Loo Wen Feng. To Dr Peter Kew, Ms Ann Yeo and Dr Percy Luu of NUS Enterprise. Mr Ahmad bin Mashadi and Ms Karen Lim, of NUS Museum, Chew Huoy Miin of NUS Office of Corporate Relations.

Special thanks to the late Associate Professor Dr Milton Tan and the DesignSingapore Council for their generous support and grants. Also special thanks to the Singapore Furniture Industries Council (SFIC), Spring Singapore and IE Singapore for their generous support and grants.

Thanks to those who have supported us in our projects: Paola Antonelli (MoMA), Murray Moss (Moss), Brigitte Silvera (Silvera), Denis Ribreau, Naoko Kubu and Shigeo Mashiro (Ricordi Sfera), Roland Lim (P5), Tristan Tan, Syddal Wee and Chin Fatt Lim (Space), Rossana Orlandi (Spazio Rossana Orlandi), Sandra Baumer and Thomas Schultz (Marron), Rumi Verjee (Thomas Goode), Denis Ribreau.

Special thanks to Ryutaro Yoshida and Asuka Ochi (Time and Style), Chantal Hamaide, Nick Vinson, Benjamin Kempton, Marva Griffin, Kelley Cheng, Jacinta Sonja Neoh, Ken Koo, Song Kee Hong, Werner Aisslinger, Boey Chee Kong, Lim Marn, Ash Yeo, Ulrich Schraudolph, Yong Jieyu, Lisa Koh, Lin Fang Wei.

Thanks to Laurence King, Ian Pringle, Amnah Tan, Abdul Basit Khan, Darryl Lim for their help in making this book possible.

This book is dedicated to the past and present members of the Design Incubation Centre's team and their families. Finally to my family for providing me with the support and inspiration.

PROFILE

Exhibitions

ACM SIGGRAPH, Vancouver, Canada; 2011
'Talk to Me', MoMA, New York, USA; 2011
Maison et Objet; Paris, France; January 2011
SaloneSatellite; Milan, Italy; April 2010
Maison et Objet; Paris, France; January 2010
P5, Singapore; November 2009
'Design for Future Mobility'; Singapore, November 2009
Ricordi & Sfera; Tokyo & Kyoto, Japan; October 2009
Japan Symposium, October 2009
SaloneSatellite; Milan, Italy; April 2009
50+ Singapore Exposition, with C3A; January 2009
Maison et Objet; Paris, France; January 2009
Time & Style; Tokyo Design Festival, October 2008
Maison et Objet; Paris, France; January 2008
National Museum, Singapore; June 2008
'Objects as Architecture, Architecture as Objects', Sculpture Square, Singapore; November 2007

Awards

Singapore President's Design Awards, Design of the Year; 2010
Red Dot Design Award, Design Concept, Experience Kaleidoscope; 2008
Red Dot Design Award, Design Concept, Dandella; 2008
Osaka Int'l Design Competition, Gold, Dandella; 2006

Selected Press Recognition

Add!ct Magazine, Belgium
Annabelle, Switzerland
Casa da Abitare, Italy
Casamica, Italy
DAMn° Magazine, Belgium
Design. China., China
Elle Decoration, United Kingdom
Frame, Netherlands
Grazia Casa, Italy
Home Concepts, Singapore
Home Décor, Singapore
Icon, United Kingdom
Intramuros, France
iSh, Singapore
Maison et Objet, Inspirations N° 15
Monocle, United Kingdom
Raum und Wohnen, Switzerland
Viewpoint Magazine, United Kingdom
Vogue, Germany
Vogue Living, Australia
Wallpaper*, United Kingdom
Wohn!Design, Germany
Singapore Architect, Singapore

Gallery Representations

Collections from d.lab have been represented by numerous galleries, shops and retailers worldwide and include:

Axis Mundi, Germany
Cream, Singapore
Galerie Gosserez, France
Graanmarkt 13, Belgium
I.T. Apparels, Hong Kong
Kunstgärtnerei Doll, Austria
La Rinascente, Italy
Le Bon Marché, France
Marron , Germany
Moss, United States
O'Driscoll, Ireland
P5, Singapore
Ricordi & Sfera, Japan
Silvera B&B Paris Store, France
Space Furniture, Australia & Singapore
Spazio Rossana Orlandi, Italy
Thomas Goode, United Kingdom

Collaborators, Partners & Participants of Our Workshops

Academia

NUS Museum
NUS Business School
NUS Interactive and Digital Media Institute
NUS Mixed Reality Lab
NUS Communications & New Media Programme
NUS School of Engineering
Centre for the Arts
Office of the Vice President (Campus Infrastructure)
National Institute of Education (NIE)
Nanyang Academy of Fine Arts (NAFA)
Temasek Polytechnic
United World College of South East Asia
Yu Neng Primary School
Dunman Secondary School

Ministries, Statutory Boards & NGOs

Ministry of Community Development, Youth and Sports
Ministry of Education
National Environment Agency
National Parks Board
Singapore Tourism Board
National Trades Union Congress
Council for Third Age
Land Transport Authority
SMRT Corporation Ltd
National Library Board
Infocomm Development Authority of Singapore
Workforce Development Agency
RSVP Singapore, Centre of Senior Volunteers
Singapore Health Services
Presbyterian Community Services
>60 Design Centre
Centre for Urban Greenery and Ecology
Institute for Infocomm Research (A*Star)

Industry

Technigroup
Asus
Design Exchange
OSA
DuPont Corian
Philips InnoHub
Designinsight
Human Network Labs
BAF Spectrum
Renewe

Editing:
  Patrick Chia
  Darryl Lim

Graphic Design:
  Terrain – Office for Research and Design
  Abdul Basit Khan and Darryl Lim
  www.terrain-rd.com

Photography:
  All Photography by Design Incubation Centre
  except for the following:
  Tajima Glass Factory (pg. 140) by Time & Style,
  Japan; Bambi Chair, Rabbit and Tortoise (pg. 191)
  and Duck Lamp (pg. 193) by Studio Juju; Purée
  de carottes (pg. 234, 235) by Marie Douel, Sine
  Shade (pg. 236, 237) by Clement Zheng

Additional texts contributions:
  Cheong Yian Ling
  Fang Siwei
  Wu Yixiu

Design Incubation Centre
Division of Industrial Design
School of Design and Environment
National University of Singapore
4 Architecture Drive, Singapore 117566
Tel: +65 6516 4881

www.designincubationcentre.com
www.dlab.com.sg
www.nusdid.edu.sg
www.sde.nus.edu.sg
www.nus.edu.sg

Design Director (DIC):
  Patrick Chia

Staff (Past and Present):
  Abdul Basit Khan
  Ang Ee Sock
  Chang Shian Wei
  Chen Huiqian
  Cheng Chee Keong
  Cheong Yian Ling
  Efrim Alexander Bartosik
  Fang Siwei
  Felix Austin
  Liu Yock Siew
  Mark Ephrem Michael
  Ng Aik Min
  Nigel Chen
  Peng Chou Kit
  Priscilla Lui
  Tay En Qi Angela
  Thiam Sai Cheong Colin
  Tiffany Loy
  Timothy Wong
  Willie Tay
  Wu Yixiu
  Yang Guoping
  Yuta Nakayama
  Yvonne Chua